HEINEMANN

GNVQ

INTERMEDIATE

Information and Communication Technology

Molly Wischhusen • Janet Snell
Andrew Scales

TUTOR'S FILE

Heinemann Educational Publishers
Halley Court, Jordan Hill, Oxford OX2 8EJ
a division of Reed Educational & Professional Publishing Ltd
Heinemann is a registered trademark of Reed Educational & Professional Publishing Ltd

OXFORD MELBOURNE AUCKLAND
JOHANNESBURG BLANTYRE GABORONE
IBADAN PORTSMOUTH (NH) USA CHICAGO

First Published 2000

03 02 01 00
10 9 8 7 6 5 4 3 2 1

A catalogue record for this book is available from the British Library
on request

ISBN 0 435 45286 X

Typeset by TA Tek-Art, Croydon, Surrey
Printed in Great Britain by Athenaeum Press, Gateshead, Tyne & Wear

Tel: 01865 888058 www.heinemann.co.uk

CONTENTS

	Page
Introduction	v
Induction – Practice material	1
Unit 1 Practice – Presenting information	
Notes to tutors	14
Student activities	15
Unit 2 Practice – Handling information	
Notes to tutors	37
Student activities	38
Unit 3 Practice – Hardware and software	
Notes to tutors	49
Student activities	51
Unit 5 Practice – Information resources	
Practice pre-release materials	74
Practice external test	76
Unit 6 Practice – Graphics	
Notes to tutors	85
Student activities	86
Units 2 & 10 (combined) Practice – Handling information and Database techniques and applications	
Notes to tutors	92
Student activities	93
Unit 2 Assessment – Handling information	
Notes to tutors	98
Assessments	100
Unit 3 Assessment – Hardware and software	
Notes to tutors	118
Assessments	118
Unit 4 Assessment – Design project	
Notes to tutors	133
Suggested topics for design projects	135
Assessments	137
Unit 6 Assessment – Graphics	
Notes to tutors	151
Assessments	151

Page

Units 2 & 10 (combined) Assessment – Handling information and Database techniques and applications
Notes to tutors 164
Assessments 166

Appendices

Appendix 1: Application forms 177

Appendix 2: Forms for designing a database 180

Appendix 3: Photographs 182

Appendix 4: Mobile Mania – scenario 183

Appendix 5: Details of the CD-ROM for the Tutor's File 185

Appendix 6: Mobile Mania – advertising material 186

Appendix 7: Timesheets 189

Appendix 8: Selecting an ICT system 193

Appendix 9: Handwritten notes of customer details 194

Appendix 10: Handwritten note from Tom to Iqbal ordering new equipment 196

Appendix 11: Letters from suppliers confirming contracts 197

Appendix 12: Two photographs for image stitching 200

Appendix 13: Fix-it shop fittings 201

Appendix 14: Key skills tracking sheets 203

Appendix 15: Answers 209

INTRODUCTION

This introduction is deliberately brief as we have included detailed 'Notes to Tutors' in each section of this *Tutor's File*, which we hope will help you make effective use of the material.

We have designed a set of practice activities to support Induction and Units 1, 2, 3, 5, 6 and 10, to correspond with the chapters in the textbook. In addition, we include assessment material for Units 2, 3, 4, 6 and 10.

PRACTICE MATERIAL

Hard copy of all practice activities is included in each section and the electronic files are also available on the CD-ROM that accompanies the resource file, as you may wish to edit the activities to suit the needs of your students. The practice material for Units 1 and 5 reflects the sample assessments we have seen, and is designed to help prepare students for the external tests in these units. It is not feasible to practise a major project and, therefore, no practice material is included for Unit 4 – Design Project.

ASSESSMENT MATERIAL

Our assessment material is based on the scenario of a mobile phone company, Mobile Mania. Our students seem to find mobile phones a never-ending source of conversation/demonstration and we hope this enthusiasm can be directed towards their work!

Please read the 'Notes to Tutors' in respect of Units 2, 4 and 10 for further detail. We believe there is scope to combine units. For example, if you are offering Unit 10 as one of your options, the material is designed *to include all the database assessment for Unit 2*. Therefore, you can omit Assessment 2.1 (the database). Suggestions for projects and how these may provide evidence for other units are explained in the notes to Unit 4.

Again, hard copy of all assessments is included and the files are also available on the CD-ROM for you to edit if you wish.

GRADING

The guidelines for grading provided by the awarding bodies indicate 'the following general qualities that distinguish between the three grades':

- increasing depth and breadth of understanding
- increasing coherence, evaluation and analysis
- increasing independence and originality
- increasing skill in the effective application of ICT.

You should, of course, check the guidelines to identify the specific requirements for each unit. However, we have included checklists with the assessments to indicate how they provide opportunities to meet the criteria for pass, merit or distinction.

APPENDICES

This section contains all supporting material for both practice and assessment, much of which has been referred to throughout the textbook. Some of the appendices are handwritten documents, but those that are in file format are available on the CD-ROM (e.g. forms used for database design, the design project, etc.). Appendix 5 gives further details of the CD-ROM.

KEY SKILLS

Tracking sheets are included, which indicate where the practice activities or assessments *may* provide evidence towards the key skills. You may wish to adapt assessments to provide further opportunities in some areas. Students undertaking a project for Unit 4 would generate evidence for 'improve own learning', but otherwise the evidence is likely to come through the tutorial programme.

CONCLUSION

We do hope you find this resource file useful, and would welcome any comments you have on those aspects that have been successful, and also those you feel need to be amended.

INDUCTION – PRACTICE MATERIAL

NOTES TO TUTORS

We have devised some activities for students to undertake during the first week or two of the new academic year. None of the activities are designed to be 'taught'. They provide opportunities for students to demonstrate their existing knowledge/skills and provide links to all three mandatory units.

Some activities require students to work together (to encourage group bonding) and some can be done individually. The activities include the following.

- *Four group activities* designed to encourage students to think about standard word processing, spreadsheet and database software and to explore the software help menus in order to discover the facilities available within the different applications. These are saved under the file reference 'Software Applications'.
- *Two individual activities* investigating the components of the computer system which encourage students to use their course textbooks, while at the same time providing the opportunity to familiarise themselves with the technical language. These are saved under the file reference 'Components'. These provide a useful introduction to Unit 3.

  If students are able to use the Internet they will find a good supply of illustrations for components and they can be encouraged to record the source of their illustrations.
- *An induction diagnostic assessment* (filename – 'Induction Assessment') comprising several activities based around the theme of an activity holiday. Resource material comprising a letter and holiday booking information are included.

  The length of induction will obviously determine the number of activities students can complete and you might, therefore, choose to ignore some of the tasks described below or use them as practice material at a later stage:
  - *Task 1* assumes the student is organising a group holiday and needs to write a few paragraphs to introduce him or herself to the rest of the group. This will give you an indication of each student's written language skills and some background information about the student. If students are able to scan their photos into their documents, it might make interesting display material for noticeboards during the first few weeks of the new term.
  - *Task 2* asks students to reply to a letter from the holiday company. This will show what existing knowledge students have about letter presentation and might provide a useful link to Unit 1.
  - *Task 3* requires the student to work out various holiday costs using a spreadsheet and provides the opportunity to use a selection of arithmetic operators – or to use a calculator if students do not know how to insert formulae. This will give an indication of their existing spreadsheet knowledge and numeracy skills. A worked example of the spreadsheet is shown below and included on the CD-ROM under the filename 'Southern Activities Centre.xls'.

Data View

Southern Activities Centre

	Price per night	Basic cost	10% deposit	Balance	Amount of each instalment	Insurance cover	Total cost
Low Season							
Weekend (3 nights)	£40.00	£120.00	£12.00	£108.00	£36.00	£17.50	£137.50
4 day break	£33.75	£135.00	£13.50	£121.50	£40.50	£17.50	£152.50
7 day holiday	£30.00	£210.00	£21.00	£189.00	£63.00	£17.50	£227.50
High Season							
Weekend (3 nights)	£44.75	£134.25	£13.43	£120.83	£40.28	£17.50	£151.75
4 day break	£39.25	£157.00	£15.70	£141.30	£47.10	£17.50	£174.50
7 day holiday	£35.00	£245.00	£24.50	£220.50	£73.50	£17.50	£262.50

Formula view

Southern Activities Centre

	Price per night	Basic cost	10% deposit	Balance	Amount of each instalment	Insurance cover	Total cost
Low Season							
Weekend (3 nights)	40	=B5*3	=C5*10%	=C5-D5	=E5/3	17.5	=C5+G5
4 day break	33.75	=B6*4	=C6*10%	=C6-D6	=E6/3	17.5	=C6+G6
7 day holiday	30	=B7*7	=C7*10%	=C7-D7	=E7/3	17.5	=C7+G7
High Season							
Weekend (3 nights)	44.75	=B10*3	=C10*10%	=C10-D10	=E10/3	17.5	=C10+G10
4 day break	39.25	=B11*4	=C11*10%	=C11-D11	=E11/3	17.5	=C11+G11
7 day holiday	35	=B12*7	=C12*10%	=C12-D12	=E12/3	17.5	=C12+G12

- *Task 4* provides an opportunity to be creative and design a handout or news-sheet for fellow students giving details of the holiday and costs. They will need to extract information from the brochure, covering letter and spreadsheet and will also have an opportunity to use Clip Art and other design tools.
- *Task 5* calls for the creation of a form for interested students to complete in order to reserve a place on the holiday. This again will allow students to use a range of word processing tools (tabs, leader dots, font styles and sizes together with use of white space, etc.). A second copy can be completed by the student by hand – this will probably lead to discussion about appropriate presentation techniques.

  We have included three worked forms as examples which could be turned into OHTs. One illustrates poor presentation techniques (Appendix 1A) and the other two show how forms can be produced using either leader dots (Appendix 1B) or tables (Appendix 1C).
- *Task 6* introduces students to evaluation and a simple table has been designed to help them evaluate the work they have completed for the Induction Assessment.
- *Task 7* offers an opportunity to design a suitable front cover for their work and provides a list of items to be handed in.

Induction Group Activity 1

Working in small groups make two lists – in one, list all the different types of software you can think of and, in the other, show brand names.

We have started the list for you.

Type of software	Brand name
Word processing	*Microsoft Word*
	Word Perfect

Induction Group Activity 2

Word processing software enables you to perform many tasks, including editing and formatting.

Working in small groups, list as many as you can under each heading. When you have finished, draw a line under your list. Now search the Help index and see if you can find any more. We have started it for you.

Editing	Formatting	Other
Correct errors	*Change font size*	*Save to disk*

Induction Group Activity 3

Spreadsheet software has many facilities to help present and process numerical data. Some apply to the **data** you enter into the spreadsheet and some to the **worksheet**.

Working in small groups, list as many as you can under each heading. When you have finished, draw a line under your list. Now search the Help index and see if you can find any more. We have started it for you.

Data	Worksheet	Other
Align text left/right/centre	*Insert columns*	*Save to disk*

Induction Group Activity 4

Database software is used for storing vast amounts of data that can be sorted or searched in different ways to provide information. For example, a library database holds details of all its books and all the members. This data becomes information when you want to find something out – for example, to find out if a particular book is in stock.

Think of businesses/organisations which regularly use a database and list them below. When you have finished, check your list with a friend's. The first one has been done for you.

Business/organisation	Description
Public library	*Holds details of all books and members and can find out who has which book and when it is due back. Public can use the database to search for a book or topic.*

Induction Individual Activity 1

A computer system comprises many components. A selection of these is listed below. Recreate this table on your computer. In column 2, indicate if the component is an input, output, storage or processing device. In column 3, try to find a picture to illustrate the component (and note the source of the graphic). In the last column, write a short description of the component and its purpose (minimum 20 words). The first one has been done for you.

Component	Type of device	Illustration	Description
Keyboard	Input	 Source: Clip Gallery Live	Used to enter data and commands into the computer. When you press a key an electrical signal is sent to the CPU. You can get different types of keyboard.
TFT LCD monitor			
Mouse			
Laser printer			
RAM			
Rollerball			
Dot-matrix printer			
DVD			
Scanner			
Floppy disk			
Visual display unit			
Digital camera			
Modem			
Ink-jet printer			
Central processing unit			
ROM			
CD writer			
Processor			
Hard disk			
Microphone/speakers			
Network card			
Ports			

Induction Individual Activity 2

To enable your computer to do anything you need software. There are many different types of software running on your computer. Recreate the table below and write a few sentences about each type of software listed in the table. You should try to write about 50 words. We have done the first one for you.

Software	Description
Computer program	A computer program is a set of instructions that make the hardware work or enables the computer to carry out a particular task. For example, when you hit the keyboard or click the mouse, the computer program interprets the command and performs the action you requested.
Word processing	
GUI	
Operating system	
Anti-virus	
ROM BIOS	
Spreadsheet	
Programming languages	
E-mail	
Desktop publishing	
Windows	
Graphics	
Personal organisers	
DOS	
Database	

INDUCTION ASSESSMENT

Welcome to the new school or college year. We have written this Induction Assessment to give you an opportunity to show us what ICT skills you already have and what you can do. Don't worry if you don't know very much at the moment – after all, that is why you are here – just do the best you can!

Scenario

You have been chosen as the new student social co-ordinator. Your role is to make sure students have opportunities to meet fellow students and to enjoy themselves while they are at your school/college. During the year you will organise many social occasions for the students, but the main event will be an activity holiday at the Southern Activities Centre during the latter part of the academic year. You have just received details about next year's holidays from the centre and these are included with this assessment.

Task 1

Your first job is to introduce yourself to the new students and to do this you have decided to write a few paragraphs telling them about yourself and your family, your last school or college, your interests and hobbies and your hopes for the future.

Produce between half to one page of A4 all about yourself. If you have the facility available to you, scan your photograph into your document.

Save the document.

Print a copy.

Task 2

The letter you have received from the Southern Activities Centre needs a reply. You must write to advise them of preferred dates for your visit and approximate numbers in your party.

At the moment you are contemplating a visit during the Easter vacation in April or towards the end of the year in June. You will probably decide on a four-day break, although you are also interested in the seven-day holiday. You anticipate your party will be made up of approximately 30–40 students plus three tutors.

Write a letter to the Southern Activities Centre, in reply to their letter, outlining your plans.

Save.

Print a copy of the letter.

Task 3

The price panel in the holiday brochure shows prices *per person per night*. Two prices are shown – the top price is the low season price and the bottom price shows the cost for the high season.

Use a spreadsheet to calculate the total holiday costs for low and high season holidays for:

- a weekend visit (3 nights)
- a 4-day break
- a 7-day holiday.

Your spreadsheet should also show the nightly price, the total cost, 10% deposit required, the balance and the amount of the three instalments. Use formulae wherever possible to calculate the costs but if you are unable to do this you can use a calculator.

Your spreadsheet will probably look something like this:

	Price per night	Basic cost	10% deposit	Balance	Amount of each instalment	Insurance cover	Total cost
Low Season							
Weekend							
4 day break							
7 day holiday							
High Season							
Weekend							
4 day break							
7 day holiday							

Use whatever tools you can to improve the appearance of your spreadsheet but don't worry if you don't yet know how to do this.

Print two copies of your spreadsheet showing both the costs and the formulae you have used (if any). Make sure you put your name on the spreadsheet, preferably in the footer.

Task 4

Now you have worked out the costs of the holiday you must produce a handout or news-sheet to give to your fellow students showing full details of the holiday. You will find all the information you need in the letter, brochure and spreadsheet. You will need to tell your fellow students how much the four-day and seven-day holidays will cost at Easter and in June so they can decide when they would prefer to go.

You should make your handout or news-sheet as interesting as possible, so be creative in your design. Make sure you include your name somewhere on your work, preferably in the footer.

Save the document.

Print a copy.

Task 5

You need a form that students who are interested in the holiday can complete to let you know which holiday they would prefer.

You will need to know their name, address and telephone number, date of birth, gender and the course they are studying at college. In addition, you might also like to find out the activities they are interested in, which holiday they prefer and whether they have any special dietary requirements (e.g. are they vegetarian?). Don't forget to include space for them to indicate when they would prefer to go and for how long.

Produce a suitable form students can complete and return to you.

Save the form and print two copies.

Fill in one copy by hand yourself.

Task 6

Before you hand the Induction Assessment in, you should prepare a brief evaluation of the work you have done to complete it.

Using your word processing software, set the page to landscape orientation and create a table of five columns and six rows. Head the columns as follows:

Task no.	ICT tools I used to complete the task	Why I chose those tools	What I might do differently if I had to do it again	What I particularly liked or disliked about this task
1				
2				
3				
4				
5				

Write something under each heading for each task you have now completed.

Make sure you put your name on the table.

Save the table.

Print a copy.

Task 7

Design a suitable front cover for your induction work using Word Art and Clip Art.

Finally, assemble your work as follows.

Assemble:

- Your front cover.
- The A4 page you have written all about yourself.
- The letter to Southern Activities Centre.
- Two copies of your spreadsheet – one with the formulae.
- The news-sheet giving details of the holiday.
- Two copies of the application form – one completed by you.
- Your evaluation of this assessment.

SOUTHERN ACTIVITIES CENTRE

Shore Farm, Sandleigh AB2 CD5

Telephone 030 6543 9876   Fax 030 6543 9879

Email mail@shorefarm.co.uk

Date as postmark

The Student Co-ordinator
Whyre College
Main Road
Whyre
RU2 4IC

Dear Visitor

SOUTHERN ACTIVITY HOLIDAYS

As requested, we have pleasure in enclosing our current adventure holiday brochure. Southern Activity Holidays are based at Sandleigh – just $1\frac{1}{2}$ miles from the sea front and $\frac{1}{4}$ mile from the town centre. Shore Farm offers comfortable accommodation in a converted stable block on a working farm. During the last 10 years Sandleigh has consistently had the best sunshine record in the area.

Our free minibus ferries visitors to local centres to pursue a selection of activities including:

swimming	sailing
mini golf	ten-pin bowling
horse riding	tennis
skating	cycling

It would be helpful if you could write and let us know the dates you are considering for your visit, together with the approximate number of visitors in your party. In this way we can hold accommodation open for you for up to 4 weeks while you organise your visit.

We look forward to hearing from you in due course.

Yours sincerely

Amanda Larkin

Enc

SOUTHERN ACTIVITIES CENTRE

BOOKING INFORMATION

terms of booking

We require a deposit of 10% at the time of booking and the balance to be paid in 3 equal instalments.

prices

LOW SEASON March/April/September/October/November
HIGH SEASON May/June/July/August

	WEEKEND Fri/Sat/Sun nights	4-DAY BREAK Mon/Tue/Wed/Thur nights	7-DAY BREAK From Saturday night
Price per person per night	£40.00 £44.75	£33.75 £39.25	£30.00 £35.00

additional benefits for groups of 10 or more

- **Free** return coach travel
- **Free** place for every 10 places booked and paid for
- Evening entertainment's programme

booking information

A 10% deposit will be requested at the time of booking.

Course price includes accommodation, full board, instruction, hire of all equipment, use of buoyancy aids, wetsuits and oilskins as appropriate. Fully qualified instructors for all activities. Free transport to activity centres.

Special dietary requirements catered for on request.

A Comprehensive Sports Insurance Policy must be taken out at the time of booking. An additional £17.50 for up to 7 days cover will be added to the cost of individual holidays. There is no reduction for short visits.

UNIT 1 PRACTICE – PRESENTING INFORMATION

NOTES TO TUTORS

The material in this section has been designed to give students the opportunity for informal and formal practice of their information presentation skills.

The informal practice consists of seven activities relating to business documents like memos, agendas, minutes etc, which are designed to develop students' experience and confidence in preparing such documents to an appropriate standard. They will also learn to identify typical features of such documents including reference, salutation, complimentary close etc. The sample documents and tasks in these practice activities are typical of the document types and tasks that we have seen as examples of the unit test.

The formal practice consists of a set of pre-release materials and a unit test, both of which have been based on sample test papers provided by Edexcel.

Activity 1.1: business letters

Task 1

Mobile Mania needs a business loan to refit its shop. Iqbal wrote the letter below to Lloyds Bank to find out how to apply. His letter contains 11 features, which are standard in business letters. Circle and name each feature. One feature – the salutation/greeting – has been done as an example.

Mobile Mania
Unit G128
Millennium Shopping Centre
Melchester, ME3 8GH

Telephone (077) 6397 6000
Fax (077) 6397 6001
E-mail mobilemania@userve.co.uk

Our ref ID/271

17 November 200-

Mr Nelson Urquart
Small Business Manager
LloydsTSB Bank plc
Southampton Row
Melchester
ME7 7RW

Dear Sir —— *Greeting/salutation*

Re: Business loans

My partner Tom Chattery and I recently established a retail outlet in the Millennium Shopping Centre selling mobile phones and other communications devices. Our business plan for this year includes re-fitting our shop and to do so we will need a business loan.

For your information, I am enclosing an advertising leaflet that will give you a clearer idea of our company. Please be kind enough to send me an information pack on your services to small businesses and a business loan application form.

Yours sincerely

Iqbal Dialup

Iqbal Dialup
Manager

Enc

Task 2

Soon after Mobile Mania set up shop, they received the letter below from a local one-man painting and decorating business. Decide what you would do to improve this letter and then rewrite it. When you have finished compare your version with somebody else's and explain why you made the changes you did.

Just the Job Paintin
123 Fairview Crescent
Melchester

Dear lads from Mowbile Mania,

How're you doing? Feelin a bit poorly meself but there you go:

I was just passing through the Mall and thought what a tatty place you've got yorselves. How about I comes over and spruces the place up a bit. I don't charge and arm and a leg and maybe you could give me a deal on one of them mowbiles.

Give me a call on 6384 5971.

Cheers,

Pat.

Activity 1.2: memos

Task 1

Look through the following memo and note:

- The position of the word 'memorandum'. Could it be placed anywhere else?
- The line across the middle of the page. Why is it there?
- The absence of a complimentary close (e.g. Yours sincerely). Why is a complimentary close unnecessary?
- Why do you think we initial memos?

Memorandum

To Issac Berlin
From Monty Evans
Date Sept 7, 200–
REF ME101

RE: Printer cabling

A customer recently caught her foot in our printer cabling, stumbled and almost fell. She was quite upset and said some very rude things to me. I have used some duct tape to secure the cable to the floor for the time being. Meanwhile, please contact those computer people – I think they're called ICT Solutions – and ask them to send someone over to do the job properly.

ME

Task 2

Now refer to the handwritten note from Tom to Iqbal in Appendix 10. Type out this note in proper memo format.

Activity 1.3: agendas

Task 1

Both Tom and Iqbal find themselves very busy trying to get their shop off the ground. Although they see each other almost every day, they usually have no time to discuss anything but immediate challenges. So that they can deal with more general issues, they decide to arrange regular meetings with a proper agenda. Here is an example:

Agenda

1 Approval of minutes from previous meeting

2 Matters arising

3 Application for business loan

4 Safety issues

5 AOB

6 Date and time of next meeting

Do you think there is anything missing from this agenda? If so, why would that be? What sort of thing do you think they might discuss under 'Matters arising'? What does 'AOB' stand for?

Task 2

After talking about safety issues for some time, Tom and Iqbal realise they don't really know much about the subject (see the minutes). So they decide to call ICT Solutions to set up a meeting to discuss safety and the use of computers in their office.

Using what you have learnt from Unit 1, draw up an agenda which ICT Solutions might set for the meeting with Mobile Mania.

Activity 1.4: minutes

Tom and Iqbal decided not to hire a secretary as they can do most of the routine office work themselves. Neither of them likes taking minutes so they decide to take turns. At the last meeting Iqbal took the minutes. Here's what he wrote:

Minutes

Mobile Mania Meeting
24 August, 200–

1 *Minutes of last meeting*: the minutes of the last meeting were read and agreed.

2 *Matters arising*: Iqbal pointed out continuing need for company logo.

3 *Application for business loan*: Tom said he has written to Lloyds to ask about loans and other services for small businesses. Iqbal asked about other banks and Tom agreed to contact Barclays and NatWest.

Action: Tom to contact two more banks.

4 *Safety issues*: Tom suggested buying a first-aid kit, just in case. Iqbal agreed but is more worried about the office computer because he had a bit of a backache last week and this week his eyes feel tired. Tom said he should get his eyes tested but Iqbal got a new pair of glasses only a month ago. Iqbal thinks there may be some laws about safety at work.

Action: Tom to ask ICT Solutions to arrange a meeting to discuss safety.

5 *AOB*: workload. It was decided that both Iqbal and Tom should stop working seven days a week and take either Saturday or Sunday as a day off.

Action: Take a day off!

6 *Date and time of next meeting*: 31 August 200-, 9 am.

Task 1

Here is another set of minutes that have had the headings removed. Read them through to see if you can prepare the agenda that led to these minutes.

MINUTES

of the meeting held at Informatics Ltd.
15 January, 200–

Present: Ms Ainsley (chair), Mr Vogel, Mr Kim, Mrs Buttersworth, Mrs Erooga

1. Mrs Pather, Mr Suzuki.

2. Approved with amendment to spelling of Mr Vogel's name.

3. None.

4. All agree that the increase of application forms means a temporary data entry clerk will be needed for two weeks, starting 1 Feb. *Action*: Mr Kim to contact Temp agency.

5. Informatics will buy a new kettle to replace the old broken one in the staffroom.

6. Some staff report that their pass cards will not open doors to the admin. area. This problem seems to have started several weeks ago. *Action*: Mrs Erooga to check access system for errors.

7. None.

8. 22 January, 10 am.

11:15 Meeting adjourned.

Activity 1.5: newsletters

The following newsletter has three of the four basic features you usually find in newsletters. List all four features and say which is missing. Then using your knowledge of document layout and presentation, make another list saying how you would make this newsletter more catchy and interesting to look at.

E-Publishing Ltd

Staff News

October 200–   Hardcopy version

EDITORIAL

Welcome to the fourteenth edition of our company newsletter. Among the interesting articles this month, you'll find an update on free remote access connections for all staff, our latest service – cinema online (don't forget your popcorn!) – and two new eComics titles. We also welcome and profile two new members of staff, Kathy and Zoran, graduates from the ICT GNVQ programme. We know it was in the air and now it's official: congrats to you-know-who on her upcoming marriage. And the regular back page 'Buy, Sell & Trade' columns. Happy reading and happy working. Ed.

Contents

Page 1	Editorial
	Remote Access
	Cinema online
	New eComics
Page 2	Welcome new staff
Page 3	Another marriage and all the photos
Back page	The Buy, Sell & Trade columns

Remote Access

Systems manager, Raad Drive, and his ICT team recently bought a new server especially to provide remote access to all staff. And it's free! A CD-Rom is available to install the latest browser on your home computer and all the connection information is ready entered. Just click 'install.exe' and follow the on-screen instructions.

Cinema online

First we brought the written word to our customers, then we brought music, now in our latest publishing adventure, we're bringing cinema online. The film makers have already been using digital media to produce their work and now that access speed is almost no problem, we're opening up the world of online movies. Check the company intranet for the first titles to be launched.

New eComics

No, not funny men, but digital comics. After the success we've had with our digital reading titles for busy, busy business people, we're launching a series of comic book titles. Like the business titles, they're available on E-Publishing's digital display book. Just touch the screen to choose a title or turn a page. With our back-lit LCD display, these eComics are great for reading in the dark!

Activity 1.6: invoices

Page 28 in the textbook lists the features usually included in invoices. Look through the following invoice and find three additional features. What are they and why do you think they are included?

E-Publishing ltd
107 Southampton Place
London WC1B 5AX

www.epublishing.com

Email:epublishing@mail.ep.uk
Tel: 020 6833 9432
Fax: 020 6833 9433

INVOICE

Attn. James Cyber
Jcyber@unixg.ac.uk

Despatch Address:
21 Doughty Street
Chesterside
C4A 2PJ
Note: All orders are dispatched on date of invoice

Order No. Internet 2023/EC104
Date & tax point 1 Feb 200-
Invoice No. 7575EC104

Item	Quantity	Unit Price	VAT at 17.5%	Total
eComic Galaxy Blasts	1	99.99	17.50	117.49
Delivery		5.34	0.93	10.33
Total due				127.82

Payment received	127.82
Balance	0.00

Authorisation No. 77-094
Mastercard
Internet Order Security 128-bit key encryption

Thank you for your business

Activity 1.7: proofreading and readability statistics

Here is a job application letter that is full of spelling, punctuation and grammar mistakes. The Flesch–Kincaid Grade level score is 9.7.

1 Begin by correcting as many mistakes as you can by hand, directly on to your hard copy of the letter.

2 Then open the file copy and use the spell checker and grammar checker to see if you found all the mistakes.

3 Try to rewrite the letter and bring the Flesch–Kincaid Grade level score down to less than 8.0.

77 Highbury
Anytown
AT1 2RJ

Mr Geoff Sooknak
Director
Web Designs Ltd
183 Main Street
London WC1B 4AX
20 April, 200–
Dear Mr Sooknak,
apprentice Web designer

I'd would like to apply for the job of Apprentice Web designer your Company and my CV is inside and this letter. This letter is explained a little bit more about myself than it is said in my CV

I've always been really into the Internet and so I has visited loads of cites in the last coupla years and nowadays I think that the good sites, the ones where the companies knows what the Web are all about and how it can developed thier businesses, are KInda similar. They have these splash pages before the detail which is prety cool and anyway, so what I want to say is that I've got a lot of expereince on the Web and a good ideas about design. So with your software, I coUld do a really great job. Please also see that it is said in my CV that I have recentely completed a course in Internet and that I've designed web pages for myself and freinds

I looking fOrward to hear from you

Yours Sincerly,

A.N. Other

Enc.

PRACTICE PRE-RELEASE MATERIALS

Candidate brief

Read the following instructions carefully. They tell you what work you must do, what you must produce and what to bring along to the external test on this unit. The work you are asked to produce will be marked along with your test and together these marks will give you a grade for the unit.

The work you do on the tasks should each have a title (e.g. Task 1, Task 2) and should include your name, your registration number, the unit name, the test date and your centre name and number.

You must bind these documents in the order they appear here.

You will be asked to prepare a set of documents to bring to the test.

These documents should be prepared so they demonstrate your ability to present information using the skills and knowledge you have learnt in this unit. You will be asked to refer to and to annotate these documents in the test. Your tutor will be asked to certify the documents you provide for the test are solely your own work.

Ensure you leave plenty of time before the test deadline to finalise and print your documents. Printers sometimes go wrong and there will be a great deal of pressure from others trying to get their work printed out! Always keep backup copies. Students who lose their work will not be able to sit the test (and will automatically fail to meet the criteria about securing their work!).

You must bring the documents to the test bound together (for example, by using a plastic spine or metal folded strips inserted through punch holes). Please do not insert them into plastic wallets or envelopes. The documents should have a cover on them with your name, your registration number, the unit name, the test date and your centre name and number.

The order of these documents is important. You must bind these documents **in the order requested**. (See list under sample documents on the next page.)

The test may draw from all aspects of the unit syllabus and you should be familiar with the assessment evidence grid. The main headings for your work are as follows:

- Write in styles that suit your readers.
- Choose and use standard layouts to present information.
- Improve the accuracy and quality of the documents you create.
- Understand some standard ways of working.
- Develop good practice in your use of ICT.

The test will ask you to write answers to questions on the documents you have brought, as well as writing answers on the question paper. This is why it is essential the documents you bring are in the right order. The test will also ask you to write on model documents contained within the test. The test may also refer directly to any of the other documents you have prepared and brought.

Questions will address your skill base: how to set up documents, to format them and lay them out. What might be the purpose of using different styles? Why you might use various features, such as line spacing, indentation, bullets, etc?

Questions will also ask you about wider knowledge and understanding. Do you understand where and why different forms of information are used? How do you validate the accuracy and sources of information? Can you justify why a particular style is right or can be improved? Do you understand confidentiality or security issues? Can you comment on the effectiveness or otherwise of particular documents?

Sample documents

As you get ready for the test you must look at the sample documents provided. There are seven of these:

1 Letter responding to a job advertisement.

2 Advertisement for a second-hand computer.

3 Business card for a gardener.

4 Fax template.

5 E-mail requesting further product information.

6 Sports club agenda.

7 Minutes of sports club.

Instructions about your preparation

Task 1

For each document you must decide:

- What they are about
- Whether they are clear
- Whether the way they are written looks right or if improvements could be made
- Identify and circle at least two bad points on each document and explain your reason.

Task 2

- For documents 2 and 3 produce hand-drawn sketches showing how you would display the documents to their full advantage.
- Produce alternatives of all seven documents to demonstrate your improvements, making sure you match the plans produced for the advertisement and business card.

Save your work.

Print.

Task 3

Write on your own copy of each document the following comments. Add to the end of each comment what you consider to be the relevant piece(s) of information:

The purpose of this document is to . . . .

The reader(s) of this documents(are) . . . .

Two good points about this document are . . . .

You will need to hand in, together with your test paper:

- The seven original documents annotated for Task 1
- Hand-drawn sketches of documents 2 and 3 for Task 2
- Your own versions of all seven documents for Task 2, annotated for Task 3.

Document 1: letter responding to a job advertisement

Febry 1st 200-
27 Sunningdale Ave
St Albans
Herts
S.A.6. 2.P.J.

Hi, my names Joe, how's it going?

I'm writing this leter to tell you that I'd like the job you were adverting in the saterday post? I don't have the kwalifictions it says but if you want you can send me on a course later.

Anyway, I'd like to start work about 10-ish if that's ok with you. Thing is I don't like getting up too early. Give us a call on the mobile (0987 1624) and we'll see about a time I can come and chat this over. I've got your adress as 187 the Crescent, St Albans and your postcode is SA9 6hw. Is that right? You better tell me or I might come to the wrong place (ha,ha).

Stay cool,

Joe McArthur.

Document 2: advertisement for a second-hand computer

Computer For Sale

1.9 Gigabyte hard drive
64 megs of ram
nice tower system
pentium 200Mhz
video and sound cards and multimedia speekers
loads of software, some of it on discs
CD ROM drive and flopy drive

Bonus: no warranty but instead I'll give you a couple of lessons and show you how to get connected to the net.

Call 0926 737 747 and speak to:

Mikey

Document 3: business card for a gardener

Gardener
Landscaping
Rubbish removal
Water features
No job to small
Roberta Flanagan
Flanaganr@mail.com
Mobile 772 5784
(no fax)
member of Green Fingers Society

Document 4: fax template

FAX

Today's **date**:
From *Kausiak Printers*
The Post House
127 Bloomingdale
Reading
RG11 3HH
Printall@eol.com

TO:-
Fax number:
Re
How many pages:-

---

type your message hear

Document 5: e-mail requesting further product information

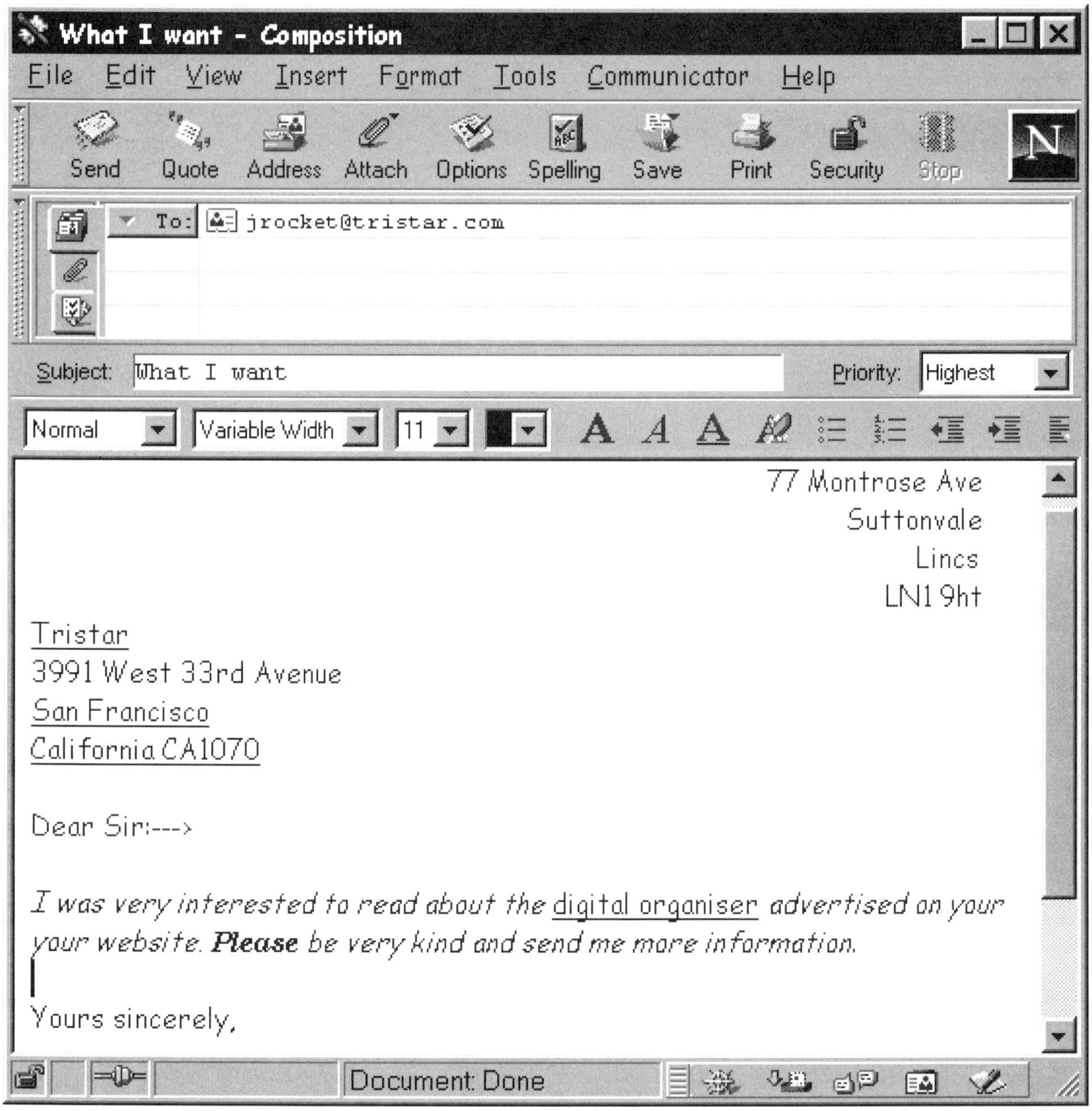

Document 6: sports club agenda

N-ER-G Programs

agenda for our next meeting
1. do we agree with last week's minutes?
2. Welcome party for new members
3. Memberships so far this year
4. Anything else we want to talk about?

Same place, same time as last week (if you've forgotten already, that's 6pm in the boss – Mrs Rees – office)

Document 7: minutes of sports club

N-ER-G Programs

Present: J. Lin, A. Pettle, Mrs Rees, J. Rekart, G. Nair. Missing: A. Athneed, CK Choi.
1. Last week's minites approved without any changes
2. Welcome party for new members: A. Pettle announced that there are lots of new member starting next month and so it might be a good idea to have a bit of a party after their orientation. All agrees. Action: G Nair to organise
3. Memberships so far this year: Mrs Rees will tell us that the cub is doing really well this year. 7 new members in january, 4 women, 3 men, 8 in February, half men half women. Then in march 6 new member 4 of them female and the other male. In april 5 new members 4 men and 1 women, and last month 12 new members 5 men and the rest women.
4. Anything else: A. Pettle says we should all get a pay rise since we're doing good business. Everyone agrees and Mrs Rees says she's gonna think about it.

J. Lin told us that the new Thai kick boxing class very popular and going well.
Same place, same time, same channel

Practice external test – Unit 1

Start time: .... Test length: 1 hour

Total marks: 100

Centre no.
Registration no.
Centre name
Last name and initials

FOR EXAMINER USE ONLY	
TOTAL MARKS	
Total	

Instructions to Candidates

In the boxes above, write your centre number and registration number, the centre name and your last name and initials.

Answer ALL questions, using the spaces provided. If you need additional space, you should continue your answers at the end of this booklet, indicating clearly which question you are answering.

Attach the detailed specification and sketch of your selected product to this booklet, as advised in the pre-release material.

TO PASS, ALL QUESTIONS MUST BE ANSWERED IN RELATION TO THE SAMPLE MATERIAL YOU HAVE WORKED ON.

TO ACHIEVE MERIT AND DISTINCTION GRADES, THERE ARE OPPORTUNITIES FOR YOU TO INCLUDE EXTRA DETAILS.

1 The following questions all relate to your new version of the letter responding to a job advertisement (document 1). Write the answers to these questions on the letter you have produced:

a Circle where you have put the recipient's address. 1
b Circle where you have put the sender's telephone number. 1
c Circle one correction you have made to the punctuation. 1
d Circle four corrections you have made to the spelling. 4
e Briefly explain any changes you may have made to the greeting at the beginning of the letter. 4
f State one way in which you have changed the style of the letter. 1

(Total 12 marks)

2 The following questions all relate to your new version of the advertisement for a second-hand computer (document 2).

a What software might you use to produce such an advertisement? 2

____

b List the formatting/design improvements you made explaining why you made these improvements. 15

____

____

____

____

____

____

(Total 17 marks)

3 The following question (a) relates to your new version of the business card for a gardener (document 3).

a Label your version of the card to show three improvements. 9
b Use the box below to sketch how you might change this card into an advertising flyer. Use text and pictures. 9

(Total 18 marks)

4 The following question relates to your new version of the fax template (document 4).

a Label three things you have done on your template to correct errors and to make the document more presentable. 6

b State the advantages of using a template for faxes. 5

(Total 11 marks)

5 The following question relates to your new version of the e-mail requesting further product information (document 5).

a Note three changes you have made and explain why. 9

(Total 9 marks)

6 The following questions relate to your new version of the sports club agenda (document 6).

a Explain the purpose of an agenda. 2

b Describe three improvements you have made to the agenda, giving your reasons why. 9

(Total 11 marks)

7 The following questions relate to your new version of the minutes of the sports club (document 7).

a On your new document, circle seven corrections you made to any of the spelling, punctuation or grammar errors. 7

b Describe two changes you made to the format of the document and why. 4

c You represented item 3 in the form of a graph. Write three advantages your graph has over textual presentation. 6

d Explain how to import a graph into a word processed document. 5

(Total 22 marks)

(Total marks for Unit 1: 100)

Practice mark scheme

Where two marks are given for any single point made, the second mark should generally be used to reflect the higher skills required for Merit or Distinction grades.

1 The following questions all relate to your new version of the letter responding to a job advertisement (document 1). Write the answers to these questions on the letter you have produced:

a Circle where you have put the recipient's address. 1
Correctly circled in an acceptable position.
b Circle where you have put the sender's telephone number. 1
Correctly circled in an acceptable position.
c Circle two corrections you have made to the punctuation. 2
Correctly circled names without apostrophe, question mark ending first sentence or the wrong use of full stops in the post code.
d Circle four corrections you have made to the spelling. 4
Any of: February, letter, Saturday, qualifications, mobile, address, advertising.
e Briefly explain any changes you made to the greeting at the beginning of the letter. 4
For example:
Too informal for this type of letter. 2
Use Dear Sir as you don't know the recipient's name. 2
f State one way in which you have changed the style of the letter. 1
For example, it should be formal not chatty.

(Total 13 marks)

2 The following questions all relate to your new version of the advertisement for a second-hand computer (document 2).

a What software might you use to produce such an advertisement? 1
Word, Publisher, purpose-built application.
Any suitable software.
b List five main changes you made explaining why. 15
Give 1 mark for each formatting/design improvement and another mark for each explanation.
A third mark for each improvement should be awarded when the work reflects distinction level.

(Total 16 marks)

3 The following questions all relate to your new version of the business card for a gardener (document 3).

a Label your version of the card to show three improvements. 9
Labelling 3 improvements,one mark each.
Sensible reasons, up to 2 marks each.
b Use the box below to sketch how you might change this card into an advertising flyer. Use text and pictures.
Quality of drawing is irrelevant.
Boxes of text, title, Clip Art/pictures – 1 mark each. 3
Layout, annotation, consideration of presentation, colour and background. Any three or similar, 2 marks each. 6

(Total 18 marks)

4 The following question relates to your new version of the fax template (document 4).

a Label three things you have done to correct errors and to make the document more presentable. 5
Stating any three things – 1 mark each.
Corrections to fonts – 2 marks.
b State the advantages of using a template for faxes. 6
Comments including: house style, ease of use/data entry, reduction of input errors or similar. Any three at 2 marks each.

(Total 11 marks)

5 The following question relates to the e-mail requesting further product information (document 5).

a Note three changes you have made and explain why. 9
Answers may include: standardising fonts, matching greeting and salutation, more appropriate statement of subject, etc. 3 marks each, 1 for changes, 2 for explanations.

(Total 9 marks)

6 The following questions relate to your new version of the sports club agenda (document 6).

a Explain the purpose of an agenda. 2
Any kind of definition around 'a list of subjects for discussion at a meeting'.

b Describe three improvements you have made to the agenda, giving your reasons why. 9
Changes may include: appropriate formal language such as substituting 'approval of previous minutes' for item 1, AOB for item 4, date and time of next meeting. Improved layout should also be taken into account.
1 mark for each improvement, up to 2 marks for explanations.

(Total 11 marks)

7 The following questions relate to your new version of the minutes of the sports club (document 7).

a On your new document, circle seven corrections you made to any of the spelling, punctuation or grammar errors. 7
1 mark for each and any of the corrections: minutes, members, agreed, full stop (after 'organise'), club, seven, January, March, members, the other two *males, April, woman, going to,* is *very popular, full stop at end.*

b Describe two changes you made to the format of the document and explain why. 4
Answers should focus on layout and readability; 2 marks for each point.

c You represented item 3 in the form of a graph. Write three advantages your graph has over textual presentation. 6
2 marks each for: readability, clarity, sequence, possibility of detecting trends or similar.

d Explain how to import a graph into a word processed document. 5
Answers are likely application specific. Mark for convincing circumstantial evidence the candidate has done this. For example, construct graph in spreadsheet program, highlight to import, have word processed document open and at correct place for insertion, use Import (or Paste), resize when placed, reformat when placed.

(Total 22 marks)

Question	Pass	Merit	Distinction	Total
1a	1			1
1b	1			1
1c	2			2
1d	4			4
1e	2	2		4
1f	1			1
2a	1			1
2b	5	5	5	15
3a	6	3		9
3b	6		3	9
4a	3	3		6
4b	3	2		5
5a	6	3		9
6a	1	1		2
6b	6	3		9
7a	7			7
7b	2	2		4
7c	3	3		6
7d	3	1	1	5
Totals	63	28	9	100

UNIT 2 PRACTICE – HANDLING INFORMATION

NOTES TO TUTORS: DATABASE

> **IMPORTANT NOTICE**
>
> **If you are planning to offer the Edexcel Option Unit 10 – Database Techniques and Applications – it would be advisable to *disregard* this practice material. The practice material for Unit 10 includes all the material for this unit with additional material to cover the requirements for Unit 10.**

Before issuing this practice activity (saved as 3Ls_dBaseU2.doc), you may find it helpful to look at the rationale behind Assessment 2.1, as the tasks are designed to follow the same pattern. As with the actual assessment material, the requirements for this database have been kept as simple as possible whilst still addressing the guidelines in the GNVQ standards. A small sample of data only has been included, since the purpose is to learn how to design, implement and search the database rather than enter data. Time for practice can be short, so the evaluation has been set as a discussion in small groups or as a whole-class activity rather than the written evaluation that will be required for the actual assessment. A model of the database is included in the CD-ROM (saved as Loose Limbs U_2).

Activity 2.1 has been divided into four stages. In our experience students may be overwhelmed by a huge assessment, and they also do prefer to get on with creating a database, ignoring the planning stages. Therefore it may be advantageous to issue the four stages separately. The four stages are as follows:

- *Part A: design* – forms for this have been included in Appendix 2.
- *Part B: implementation*. A field for 'gender' has been included in the database. The students will probably not include this field, as it is not obvious from the data provided. This is deliberate so that when they reach Task 8, which requires a list of lady members, they will have to amend their database design.
- *Part C: entering/saving data and searching for information* The reports required for Tasks 5, 6 and 7 are included in the database model, but not Tasks 8 and 9 as these reports necessitate changes to the original file:

  Task 8 – to make this search the students will have to delete a record and probably amend the design of the database and include a male/female field.

  Task 9 – to make this search the two records will need to be changed.
- *Part D: evaluating the database.*

Activity 2.1

Scenario

The 3L's Club (Loose Limbs Leisure) has recently installed a computer system and has approached ICT Solutions Ltd to design a database to keep track of members' details and trainers' details. You have been given the task of planning, designing and implementing a suitable relational database. Currently the details are written in a card index system and if so include the following information.

Members' details

Membership number, title, last name, first name, address (street), town, post code, telephone number, date of birth. Also included is whether they use a private trainer and if so the trainer's ID.

Trainers' details

Trainer's ID, title, last name, first name, telephone number, category, hourly rate.

Part A: design

Task 1

Use the two copies of Form A to plan the design of a suitable database file which will provide *two related tables*, 'Members' and 'Trainers'.

Look back to the section on 'Setting up a computerised database' in Unit 2 on page 74. Think carefully about the following:

- The primary key for each table. (The members need a unique membership number, which may be created as a field with a *sequenced counter*, so each new member is automatically given the next number in the sequence. The trainers also need a unique ID which is based on a three-digit code using their initials.)
- How these two tables can be linked together.
- Any other fields that may be useful.
- The length and type of field – consider carefully the best way to design the fields.
- Which of those fields would be secondary keys (indexed).
- Whether you could use a range check.
- Whether a field should be required or not.

Using Form B, explain in one or two sentences why you have chosen each *different type* of field. For example, if several fields are text fields you can give *one* explanation for choosing text for all the text fields.

Part B: implementation

Task 2

Save all your work for this activity in the database subdirectory/folder called Practice you created for Unit 2 (see page 151 in the textbook) using a suitable file name.

Having planned the design of your database, you are now ready to set up the two tables using the database software.

Build the relationship between the two tables.

Print the relationship form.

Print the design details for both tables.

Note: If you are using Microsoft Access 97, to print the table design requested, select the Tables **Tables** tab and from the **Tools** menu choose:

Analyzer, Documenter, Options and then select the boxes illustrated

(For Access version 2, select **File, Add-ins, Database Documenter**)

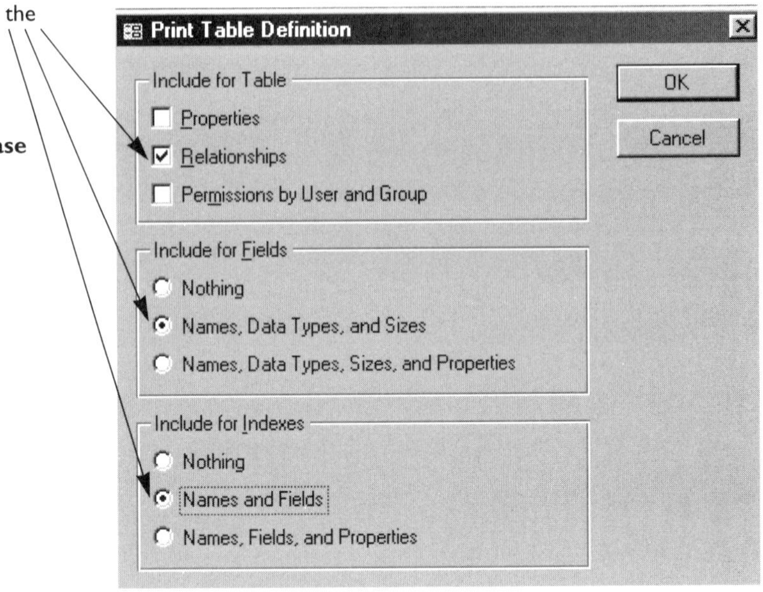

Task 3

From the tables, create the **Form** view.

If the software you are using is suitable, enhance the form design as you feel fit (e.g. use suitable fonts, point size, a heading, colour, shading). The form design should *not* occupy more than one screen page.

Print a copy of the form for both tables.

Save the file.

Part C: entering/saving data and searching for information

Task 4

Using the data supplied, enter the relevant details into both the Members' Table and the Trainers' Table. *Include your own name and address and choose a personal trainer.* Accurate data entry is essential so *proof read* each record *carefully* to check for errors.

Print one report showing all records of members, sorting them in *ascending* order of membership ID, and a second report showing the trainers' details in *descending* order of rate of pay.

Before you print **check** whether:

- The columns are wide enough to see all the data.
- The Members' Table will fit on one screen page, if necessary adjusting the margins.

Annotate the printout to explain how you designed your query.

> ***Note:* For each of Tasks 5–10, produce a report from the query *indicating the task number and your own name in the header.***

Task 5

Print a list of all members' names in order of their date of birth, showing name and date of birth only.

Annotate the printout to explain how you designed your query.

Task 6

The secretary wishes to find out which members are *not* using a personal trainer, so that a mail shot can be sent to them promoting the service.

Print a report giving a list of the title, names and addresses of relevant members only.

Annotate your printout to explain how you designed your query.

Task 7

The secretary also wishes to check which members are using the tennis trainer.

Print a report showing the name of the tennis coach *only*, and the names of relevant members.

Annotate your printout to explain how you designed your query.

Task 8

Mrs Vanderwall has moved to Manchester, so delete her record from the file.

Print a report showing the names of *lady* members *only* in alphabetical order.

Annotate your printout to explain how you designed your query.

Task 9

Ms Wainwright has married Mr Albridge and their new address is 23 Merryview Court, ANYTOWN, AN6 7VC and their new telephone number is 016 6317 9001.

Print a report of these two records *only*.

Annotate your printout to explain how you designed your query.

Task 10

Make sure your database is saved in the *relevant directory/folder* with a *suitable filename*. Make a backup copy of the file and print screen dumps showing the file saved on the hard drive and the floppy disk.

Part D: evaluating the database

Task 11

For your actual assessment you will need to write an evaluation of your database. However, for this practice activity, discuss the evaluation with other students, either in small groups or as a whole class to compare the following points:

- Explain any problems you encountered in the design of your database and any changes you have made, or would like to make, to improve the design.
- Did you have to amend your design to include any searches?
- Which further fields or tables would improve the effectiveness of the database?
- Did you find creating a database easy/difficult, simple/complex?
- Bearing in mind you were probably inexperienced in database design, how satisfied are you with the final result?
- Any other considerations you consider important or necessary.

Members' details

Member No.	Title	Last name	First name	Address	Town	Post code	Telephone	Date of Birth	Date joined	Private Trainer	Trainer ID
1	Ms	Wainwright	Jean	95 Stow Hill	ANYTOWN	SA4 6TX	(016) 6563 3144	20/02/71	12/02/95	Yes	BRJ
2	Mr	Nicholls	James	45 Crown St	ANYTOWN	AN1 5TV	(016) 6674 3198	14/03/50	20/01/92	Yes	JKG
3	Mrs	Nicholls	Anne	45 Crown St	ANYTOWN	AN1 5TV	(016) 6674 3198	20/08/52	20/04/92	Yes	SMC
4	Miss	Nicholls	Rachel	45 Crown St	ANYTOWN	AN1 5TV	(016) 6674 3198	09/05/90	20/05/00	No	
5	Mr	Patel	Prashant	24 The Close	ANYTOWN	AN6 4EH	(016) 6342 7145	12/11/60	24/03/95	Yes	JKG
6	Miss	Wong	Kim	17 Church Drive	ANYTOWN	AN5 7GH	(016) 6212 5689	12/03/85	30/10/92	No	
7	Mr	Phillips	Dwayne	33 Pine Avenue	ANYTOWN	AN4 6GD	(016) 6212 3221	23/10/65	07/09/89	Yes	BRJ
8	Mrs	Phillips	Charmaine	33 Pine Avenue	ANYTOWN	AN4 6GD	(016) 6212 3221	19/12/66	07/09/89	Yes	MKF
9	Miss	Phillips	Leona	33 Pine Avenue	ANYTOWN	AN4 6GD	(016) 6212 3221	01/02/90	16/12/99	No	
10	Mr	Albridge	Samuel	16 Inwood Close	ANYTOWN	AN9 3BV	(016) 6443 7821	09/08/69	16/06/91	Yes	BDS
11	Mrs	Vanderwall	Louise	24 William St	ANYTOWN	AN2 2GH	(016) 6674 4901	14/09/55	21/07/86	Yes	MKF
12	Your own name and details										

Trainers' details

Trainer's ID	Title	Last Name	First Name	Telephone	Category	Hourly Rate
BDS	Mr	Sonecha	Bharat	(016) 2578	Karate	£12.00
BRJ	Ms	Bronwen	Jenkins	(016) 7474	Tennis	£15.00
JKG	Mr	James	Goodman	(108) 4666	Golf	£16.00
MKF	Miss	Mary	Fitzgerald	(016) 3190	Swimming	£12.00
SMC	Mrs	Sew	Ch'ng	(018) 3198	Aerobics	£14.00

NOTES TO TUTORS: SPREADSHEET

Practice Activity 2.2 (saved as Quality_Hi-Fi.doc) has been designed to enable students to use the various functions required for the Spreadsheet Assessment 2.2, including relative and absolute cell references. The activity has been divided into four sections:

- Part A: designing the spreadsheet.
- Part B: entering the data.
- Part C: creating graphs.
- Part D: evaluation.

It might be advisable to issue part A separately to check the template is a reasonable working model before students attempt to enter the data. Time for practice can be short, so the evaluation has been set as a discussion in small groups or as a whole-class activity rather than the written evaluation which will be required for the actual assessment.

Three versions of the spreadsheet are included in the resource material:

1 Sales.xlt – a poorly laid out template, shown below, has been prepared for students to use, with no formulae or any attempt at adding borders or shading to enhance the layout (Task 1).

	A	B	C	D	E	F	G	H	I	J	K	L
1	Sales This Month											
2										Rate of co	1.50%	
3	Region	Store	Sales Assi	Videos	TVs	Cameras	Camcorde	Total Sales	Goods Ret	Net Sales	Comm.	Bonus
4	South	01	Gannon Michael									
5		02	Patel Bharat									
6		03	Brown Jane									
7		04	Gannon Megan									
8			Total									
9	North	05	Ahmed Sidika									
10		06	Williams John									
11		07	Ling Yin									
12		08	Evans James									
13			Total									
14			Grand Total									

2 Sales2.xlt – a model template layout that includes the formulae for total and net sales, commission and bonus (Task 2).

	A	B	C	D	E	F	G	H	I	J	Formula Bar	L
1						**Sales This Month**						
2								**Rate of commission =:**			**1.50%**	
3	**Region**	**Store**	**Sales Assistan**	**Videos**	**TVs**	**Cameras**	**Camcorders**	**Total Sales**	**Goods Returns**	**Net Sales**	**Comm.**	**Bonus**
4	**South**	01	Gannon Michael					0		0	0	0
5		02	Patel Bharat					0		0	0	0
6		03	Brown Jane					0		0	0	0
7		04	Gannon Megan					0		0	0	0
8			**Total**	**0**	**0**	**0**	**0**	**0**	**0**	**0**	**0**	**0**
9	**North**	05	Ahmed Sidika					0		0	0	0
10		06	Williams John					0		0	0	0
11		07	Ling Yin					0		0	0	0
12		08	Evans James					0		0	0	0
13			**Total**	**0**	**0**	**0**	**0**	**0**	**0**	**0**	**0**	**0**
14			**Grand Total**	**0**	**0**	**0**	**0**	**0**	**0**	**0**	**0**	**0**
15												

	B	C	D	E	F	G	H	I	J	K	L
3	Sto re	Sales Assista	Videos	TVs	Cam eras	Ca mco	Total Sales	Go od	Net Sales	Comm.	Bonus
4	01	Gannon Michael					=SUM(D4:G4)		=H4-I4	=J4*K2	=IF(J4>8000,30,0)
5	02	Patel Bharat					=SUM(D5:G5)		=H5-I5	=J5*K2	=IF(J5>8000,30,0)
6	03	Brown Jane					=SUM(D6:G6)		=H6-I6	=J6*K2	=IF(J6>8000,30,0)
7	04	Gannon Megan					=SUM(D7:G7)		=H7-I7	=J7*K2	=IF(J7>8000,30,0)
8		Total	=SUM(D4:D7)	=SUN	=SUI	=SUI	=SUM(H4:H7)	=SU	=SUM(J4:J7)	=SUM(K4:K7)	=SUM(L4:L7)
9	05	Ahmed Sidika					=SUM(D9:G9)		=H9-I9	=J9*K2	=IF(J9>8000,30,0)
10	06	Williams John					=SUM(D10:G10)		=H10-I10	=J10*K2	=IF(J10>8000,30,0)
11	07	Ling Yin					=SUM(D11:G11)		=H11-I11	=J11*K2	=IF(J11>8000,30,0)
12	08	Evans James					=SUM(D12:G12)		=H12-I12	=J12*K2	=IF(J12>8000,30,0)
13		Total	=SUM(D9:D12)	=SUN	=SUI	=SUI	=SUM(H9:H12)	=SU	=SUM(J9:J12)	=SUM(K9:K12)	=SUM(L9:L12)
14		Grand Total	=D8+D13	=E8+I	=F8+	=G8+	=H8+H13	=I8+	=J8+J13	=K8+K13	=L8+L13

(Sales2.xlt – Formula view)

3 Neat-Sales.xls – a model layout after data has been entered. See next page for graphs (Task 6). To create the graphs instructions for copying cells containing formulae have been included. These apply to Excel, which you may need to revise depending on the software available. This model layout can be given to students *after* they have completed their own version to check if their results are accurate and to compare their layout (Task 3).

	A	B	C	D	E	F	G	H	I	J	K	L
1	Sales This Month											
2								Rate of commission =:			1.50%	
3	Region	Store	Sales Assista	Videos	TVs	Cameras	Camcorders	Total Sales	Goods Returne	Net Sales	Comm.	Bonus
4	South	01	Gannon Michael	2000	4500	800	4050	11350	200	11150	167.25	30
5		02	Patel Bharat	1800	1060	950	1200	5010	350	4660	69.9	0
6		03	Brown Jane	2350	1890	840	3400	8480	1000	7480	112.2	0
7		04	Gannon Megan	3200	500	950	4800	9450	450	9000	135	30
8			Total	9350	7950	3540	13450	34290	2000	32290	484.35	60
9	North	05	Ahmed Sidika	1875	890	750	3600	7115	1200	5915	88.725	0
10		06	Williams John	2360	1450	840	3800	8450	700	7750	116.25	0
11		07	Ling Yin	2400	1290	560	4790	9040	300	8740	131.1	30
12		08	Evans James	2860	650	420	3899	7829	350	7479	112.185	0
13			Total	9495	4280	2570	16089	32434	2550	29884	448.26	30
14			Grand Total	18845	12230	6110	29539	66724	4550	62174	932.61	90

(Neat–Sales.xls)

4 New-Rate.xls – showing the changes after the commission rate has been increased (Task 5).

Sales This Month

Rate of commission =: 2.00%

Region	Store	Sales Assistant	Videos	TVs	Cameras	Camcorders	Total Sales	Goods Returned	Net Sales	Comm.
South	01	Gannon Michael	2000	4500	800	4050	11350	200	11150	223
	02	Patel Bharat	1800	1060	950	1200	5010	350	4660	93.2
	03	Brown Jane	2350	1890	840	3400	8480	1000	7480	149.6
	04	Gannon Megan	3200	500	950	4800	9450	450	9000	180
		Total	**9350**	**7950**	**3540**	**13450**	**34290**	**2000**	**32290**	**645.8**
North	05	Ahmed Sidika	1875	890	750	3600	7115	1200	5915	118.3
	06	Williams John	2360	1450	840	3800	8450	700	7750	155
	07	Ling Yin	2400	1290	560	4790	9040	300	8740	174.8
	08	Evans James	2860	650	420	3899	7829	350	7479	149.58
		Total	**9495**	**4280**	**2570**	**16089**	**32434**	**2550**	29884	597.68
		Grand Total	**18845**	**12230**	**6110**	**29539**	**66724**	**4550**	**62174**	**1243.48**

5 Graphs – Task 6

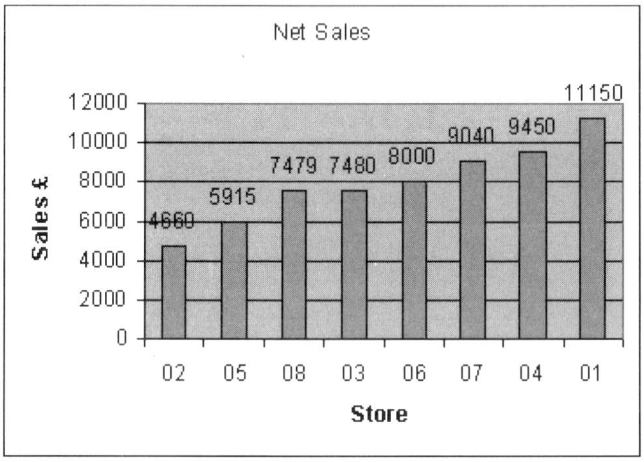

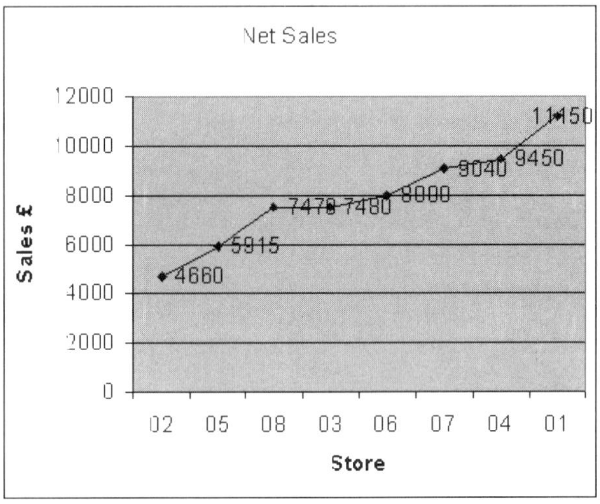

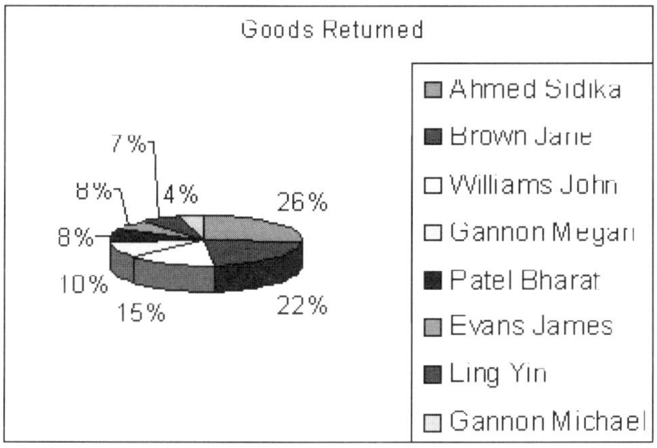

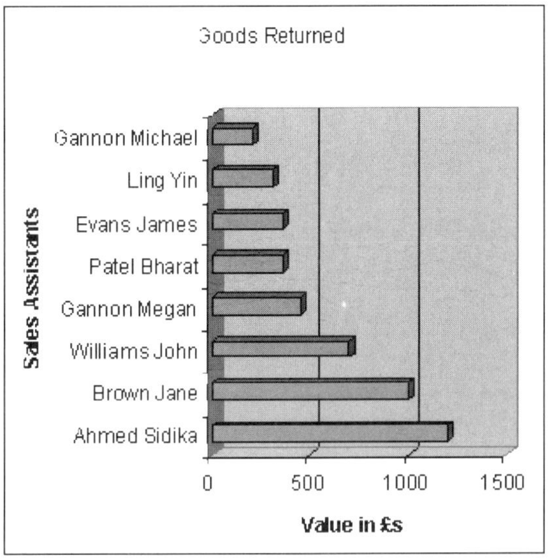

Activity 2.2

Scenario

Quality Hi-Fi Ltd have four stores in the north and four in the south. The sales staff in the stores are paid a salary, but also earn commission on the goods they sell. The sales manager wishes to keep track of the following:

- Sales each assistant makes on videos, TVs, cameras and camcorders.
- Value of returned goods for each assistant.
- Commission earned by each assistant.
- Total sales, returns and commission for north and south stores.
- Total of all sales, returns and commission.

Part A: designing the spreadsheet

Task 1

Save all your work for this activity in the spreadsheet directory/folder you created for Unit 2 (see page 151 in textbook) using a suitable file name. Copy the file saved as **Sales.xlt** into it. *Open* it as a *template* file.

Add your own name to the file footer (the filename and date are already entered).

Task 2

a Insert a formula in cell H4 to calculate the total sales for Store 01, and copy the formula down rows 5 to 7 and 9 to 12.

b Insert a formula in Cell J4 to calculate the net sales for Store 01 by taking away the goods returned from the total sales, and copy the formula down rows 5 to 7 and 9 to 12.

c Insert a formula in cell K4 to calculate the commission earned by multiplying the net sales by the rate of commission *using an absolute cell reference*, and copy the formula down rows 5 to 7 and 9 to 12.

d A bonus of £30 is paid for net sales over £8,000. Insert a formula in cell L4 to calculate any bonus earned using the 'If function'. Copy the formula down now 5 to 7 and 9 to 12.

e Insert formulae in cells D8, D13 and D14 to calculate the total sales for videos for the south and north regions and the grand total. Copy these formulae across columns E to L.

f Improve the appearance of the layout using the skills you developed in Unit 2, Section 2.3 (Spreadsheet methods Page 81). Use borders and shading rather than gridlines to improve the appearance. Try to keep as much of the spreadsheet as possible visible within one screen page.

g Make sure your name, the date and the filename are in the footer and the sheet name is in the header.

🖫 *Save* the file as a *template* file called **Sales2.xlt**

h *Centre* the spreadsheet neatly on the page.

🖶 *Print two copies* of the *template,* one showing the *formulae* used. Close the file.

✎ *Annotate* the printout to explain the formulae.

> *Note:* At this stage it is vital you show your printouts to your teacher/tutor for checking, as correct answers to the following tasks depend on the template being correct!

Part B: entering the data

Task 3

a Enter the sales figures as shown below:

Region	Store	Sales Assistant	Videos	TVs	Cameras	Camcorders	Total Sales	Goods Returned
South	01	Gannon Michael	2000	4500	800	4050		200
	02	Patel Bharat	1800	1060	950	1200		350
	03	Brown Jane	2350	1890	840	3400		1000
	04	Gannon Megan	3200	500	950	4800		450
North	05	Ahmed Sidika	1875	890	750	3600		1200
	06	Williams John	2360	1450	840	3800		700
	07	Ling Yin	2400	1290	560	4790		300
	08	Evans James	2860	650	420	3899		350

Save the file as a **Workbook** file called **Neat-Sales.xls**

b Proofread your work *carefully* to check for any errors.

Print a copy of the spreadsheet.

Task 4

Ask your tutor for a completed version of the spreadsheet.

a Check whether the results of your formulae match and if not correct any errors.

b Compare your layout with the master copy and make any improvements you think necessary.

Task 5

The business is going so well the Sales Manager thinks he can increase the rate of commission to 2%. *Amend* the spreadsheet.

Save the file as **New-Rate.xls**

Print a copy of the *spreadsheet.*

Annotate the printout to explain the effect of the change in commission.

Part C: creating graphs

Task 6

The Sales Manager would like to see various comparisons illustrated as graphs or charts.

a Open the *original* file **Neat-Sales.xls** and insert two new worksheets called **Graphs and Graphs2.**

b Copy the heading *Store* and the *store numbers* on to the worksheet **Graphs** and also the heading *Net Sales* and the *sales values.*

If you are using Excel highlight the first section and then hold the *CTRL* key, then highlight the next section and so on. This allows you to copy non-adjacent cells.

Switch to the sheet for **Graphs** and select **Edit, Paste**.

c Sort the sales figures in ascending order.

d Create both a column chart and a line graph to compare the net sales for each of the stores. Make sure you:

- remove the legend
- include a chart title – **Net Sales**
- include the category title – **Store** – and the value title – **Sales £**.

Print both graphs.

Annotate the printouts to indicate which version you feel best illustrates the data.

e Using the same method for (**b**) above, copy the heading **Sales Assistant** and their *names*, and the heading **Goods Returned** and the *values* into the worksheet **Graphs 2.**

f Create a pie chart showing the *percentage* of goods returned and add a chart title – **Goods Returned.**

g Using the same data create a bar chart showing the *values*. Remove the legend and add a chart title – **Goods returned** – and also a category title – **Sales Assistants** – and a value title – **Value in £s.**

Print both graphs.

Annotate the printouts to indicate which version you feel best illustrates the data.

Part D: evaluation

Task 7

For your actual assessment you will need to write an evaluation of your spreadsheet. For this practice activity, discuss the evaluation with other students, either in small groups or as a whole class to compare the following points:

- What changes have you made to the original sales template?
- Do these changes make it easier to use the spreadsheet?

UNIT 3 PRACTICE – HARDWARE AND SOFTWARE

NOTES TO TUTORS

Unit 3 introduces students to hardware and software, programming and setting up a system. We have produced worksheets designed to familiarise students with the components of a computer system. These activities follow on from the individual induction activities. They can be introduced in any order – for example you might prefer to issue 3.5 before 3.3 and 3.4.

Activity 3.1 (Adverts.doc) shows four advertisements and students are asked to identify the differences in the four systems and suggest who potential users of each system might be. We have included a guide which indicates the differences we had in mind when designing the activity. It should provide the opening for some discussion about the components in a computer system.

Activity 3.2 (Yourspec.doc) shows the components that Yourspec Computers will put together to build a system. We have included a series of scenarios where students can specify the components to match the user – it is hoped these will enable students to consider a wide range of user needs. A separate section outlines our thoughts in designing this exercise. Students can also specify their own ideal computer.

The opportunity to set up a macro and template is provided through activities 3.3 and 3.4.

Activity 3.3 (Macro.doc) suggests students set up a macro to insert and format a table. They are asked to write brief user instructions for using the macro and to ask a friend to try to run the macro working from their instructions.

Activity 3.4 (Template.doc) suggests students design a template to be used as a front cover for their assessments. They are asked to design the template by hand and show sufficient instructions to enable a friend to set it up for them. When they have created their own template it is suggested they hand their designs to a friend (and vice versa) to see if the instructions were clear enough to enable somebody else to design it as they intended. Again, we have suggested brief user instructions are written and given to the friend to see if he or she can use the template.

System configuration is difficult to cover since students nationally may not all be using the same software and school or college restrictions may make it difficult for them to undertake a range of activities. The worksheets we have created return to the theme in the textbook where students were encouraged to look and find out for themselves. They are designed to provide an opportunity for class discussion.

Activity 3.5 (Config1.doc) is a simple exercise designed to make students think about setting a system up and they are asked to put a list of activities in the right order.

Activity 3.6 (Config2.doc) gives students the opportunity to investigate the Control Panel and to record any questions they have on a separate sheet which can be used in a class discussion.

Activity 3.7 (Config3.doc) is a similar activity investigating applications system configuration.

Activity 3.8 (html1.doc) asks students to study some pages of html code and identify the tags and anchors, etc., they were introduced to in the textbook. Although the code is complex it will open up some interesting discussion.

Activity 3.9 (html2.doc) asks students to design their own web pages about their course and their friends. It is hoped that it will be possible for all the students to save their personal web pages on the same part of the school or college network so they can access each other's and create hyperlinks from their pages. However, it is recognised this may be difficult and students might therefore need to put copies of their friends' html files into their own area.

Activity 3.1 NOTES TO TUTORS

The notes below identify the differences that we had in mind when designing this practice material.

HiShot RW	Maestro Plus
• Ideal for home photography with camera and image editing software included. • Better graphics card. • CD re-writer to store photos on CD. • Colour printer.	• Basic system but high specification. • No extra peripherals. • Probably suit experienced user who wants a fast system but is not interested solely in games.

Strategy 3	Video Master P
• Suggested starter pack for the family. • Good basic specification. • Budget processor. • Probably used for games for children (only CD-ROM). • Maybe basic home use.	• The home entertainment system. • Ideal for videos/games. • TV facility. • Very high specification. • Large screen. • Fast graphics card. • Good sound system. • Price does not include printer, etc.

Activity 3.1

Illustrated below are advertisements for four computer systems. Compare the systems to identify the differences in the specifications. On the following page describe the type of computer user who might be attracted to each computer system.

HiShot RW

Intel Celeron 500 MHz Processor
64 MB SDRAM
13GB hard disk drive
17" SVGA colour monitor
64 MB graphics card
DVD ROM/CD re-writer
3.5" floppy drive
Stereo speakers
56k modem
Kodak Zoom digital camera and image editing software
Gamepad/colour jet printer/300 dpi flatbed scanner
Microsoft Windows/Works

Price £986.43 ex VAT (£1199.00 inc VAT)

Maestro Plus

600 MHz AMD Athlon Processor
64 MB SDRAM
20 GB hard disk
17" non-interlaced SVGA screen
32 MB graphics card
DVD ROM drive
56k modem with fax/internet
3.5" drive
Soundminder Sound
Microsoft Windows 98
Smartsuite Millennium

Price £799.00 ex VAT (£978.78 inc VAT)

Strategy 3

500 MHz AMD Processor
32 MB SDRAM
4.3 GB hard disk
15" SVGA screen
32 × CD ROM drive
56k modem for fax/internet
3.5" drive
3D standard stereo
300 jet printer/flatbed scanner
Microsoft Windows 98
Smartsuite Millennium
Indoor digital camera
5 extra games

Price £645.00 ex VAT (£797.83 inc VAT)

Video Master P

Intel Pentium III 800 MHz
256 MB SDRAM
40 GB hard disk
19" non-interlaced SVGA screen
32 MB 3D graphics card
DVD ROM drive/3.5" drive
TV tuner with Teletext
CD re-writer
56k modem
Super Soundblast Sound
Microsoft Windows 98
Microsoft Works Suite 2000
Gamepad

Price £1497.06 ex VAT (£1799.00 inc VAT)

HiShot RW	Maestro Plus

Strategy 3	Video Master P

Activity 3.2 NOTES TO TUTORS

This exercise has been designed to give students the opportunity to choose components to match different user requirements.

We have not given 'answers' since a suitable system specification could have several variations. However, the following notes outline our thinking behind the different scenarios:

- **Tom** (the architect) will obviously need CAD software and a powerful processor/large hard drive to handle his work. A large screen would be beneficial and he would probably find a CD-RW useful. He should be able to produce high-quality prints of his drawings. E-mail might be useful to keep in touch with his clients/contractors. Anti-virus software should always be specified.
- **Ketan** (the dentist) – use of a database for patient records and scheduler for appointments and reminders. He might find a digital camera useful to provide a record of patients' teeth before and after treatment. CD-RW to back up? Internet connection to keep up to date with dental research, etc., through Royal College of Dental Practitioners. TFT LCD screen would be stylish for reception desk. Must have anti-virus software because of access to the Internet.
- **Fiona** (the home typist) – ergonomic keyboard should be specified here in view of her RSI symptoms. A low-spec system since main use will be word processing. Floppy drive to put students' work on disk. A cordless mouse might be easier to use as she could use it on her lap to help alleviate the RSI symptoms? Anti-virus software in case she uses disks brought to her by students. A scheduler might help her keep track of deadlines.
- **Fred** (the editor) needs a system capable of handling large graphic files. Scanner essential together with top quality colour printer and large screen. He might find digital camera useful. DTP and graphics software essential. E-mail will enable him to receive contributions to magazine electronically. Anti-virus software essential if receiving e-mails.
- **Carlton** (the games enthusiast) will need a joystick or might like a rollerball. Best speakers for sound effects and large screen for optimum impact. Modem to enable him to link up over the Internet with other games enthusiasts. Definitely CD-Rom and DVD-Rom. Anti-virus software.
- **Tanushka** (the art student) will need additional graphics software and probably a scanner and colour printer. Digital camera might also be useful for her and Internet access for research is essential. Anti-virus software in view of Internet access and the strong possibility of using disks at college and at home. As she will probably have e-mail at college it may not be essential at home.
- **Scott** (the photographer) – obviously digital camera(s) and supporting graphics software. Large screen with large capacity hard drive and fast processor. Will need a CD-RW to store his films. Top-quality printer.
- **Callum** (who likes music and films) will need modem in order to use Internet and will require software that enables him to produce html files – standard Office Suite provided may not do this. Large screen and DVD to watch films and CD-RW to record music he finds on the Internet. Best-quality speakers to benefit both sound tracks of films and music. Anti-virus software essential.
- **Trevor** (the accountant) – first impressions will be important to his clients and therefore TFT LCD screen and electronic diary to record client's appointments in reception will be impressive. Will need to acquire professional office software and possibly specialist accounting software. Will need access to Internet to keep up to date with financial markets and anti-virus software (particularly as clients will bring their disks to him).
- **Jake** (with physical disabilities) might find a concept keyboard programmed to suit his particular requirements very useful. Voice recognition software would also be beneficial to him and therefore he would need microphone and speakers. Large screen might be helpful. As Jake has physical and not mental disabilities he might also find the Internet useful together with ability to use CDs and DVDs.
- **Final** column is left blank for students to describe, specify and justify their own ideal computer.

YOURSPEC COMPUTERS

You choose
We build your computer to match your specification!

Choose from our extensive list of components to suit your particular needs. Tick the last column to indicate your choice and circle the particular specification where appropriate.

COMPONENT		SPECIFICATION	✓
Casing		Desktop/Mini Tower/Tower	
Keyboard		Natural/Ergonomic/Concept	
Mouse		Traditional/Cordless/Optical	
Roller Ball			
Scanner		300/600/700/1000/1200 dpi	
Microphone			
Digital Camera			
Memory	Hard Disk	6/8.4/10/13/17/20/27/40 GB	
	RAM	64/128/252 MB	
Processor		Celeron 500 MHz	
		AMD 450/500/550 Mhz	
		Pentium III 550/600/700/800 MHz	
Drives		Floppy	
		CD	
		CD-RW	
		DVD	
Modem			
VDU	Monitor	15"/17"/19"	
VDU	TFT LCD	15"/17"/19"	
Printer	Laser	1400 dpi/17 ppm 1200 dpi/10 ppm	
	Ink Jet	1000 dpi/6 ppm 1200 dpi/10 ppm	
Speakers		Stereo 32/Stereo 64/Sub Woofer	

All computers come ready installed with the standard Office Suite software package for word processing, spreadsheets and databases.

Activity 3.2

Yourspec Computers have been busy advertising their business and people are very interested in designing computer systems to their own specification. The table below lists several people who are considering buying new computer systems. Using Yourspec's advertisement, suggest the components they should put together to make a suitable system. The first one has been done to help you.

	Harry has just retired and wants a computer to 'try it out' and have a look at the Internet.	Tom is an architect who wants to produce plans on the computer rather than drawing them by hand.	Ketan has just taken over a dental practice. Everything is done manually and he wants to bring it up to date.
Casing	*Any*		
Keyboard	*Natural*		
Mouse	*Traditional*		
Rollerball	✗		
Scanner	✗		
Microphone	✗		
Digital camera	✗		
Hard disk	*6 GB*		
RAM	*64 MB*		
Processor	*Celeron 500 MHz*		
Drives	*Floppy*		
Modem	*Yes*		
VDU	*17"*		
Printer	*Ink jet 1000 dpi/6 ppm*		
Speakers	*Stereo 32*		
Software	*Standard*		
Justification	*A very basic model but adequate for a beginner's needs. A larger screen in case Harry's eyes are not too good!*		

	Fiona wants to start a business at home typing dissertations for students. She has just developed RSI symptoms.	Fred is to be editor of a new in-house magazine for a travel company. The magazine will be full of travel pictures to promote the company.	Carlton is really keen on playing computer games and is going to get a new computer for his birthday.
Casing			
Keyboard			
Mouse			
Rollerball			
Scanner			
Microphone			
Digital camera			
Hard disk			
RAM			
Processor			
Drives			
Modem			
VDU			
Printer			
Speakers			
Software			
Justification			

	Tanushka is an art student who needs a computer to produce her work and to help her with research.	Scott is a photographer who enjoys still and video photography and who wants to have a go at producing some amateur films.	Callum is heavily into music and films. He wants to set up a web page and find music on the Internet.
Casing			
Keyboard			
Mouse			
Rollerball			
Scanner			
Microphone			
Digital camera			
Hard disk			
RAM			
Processor			
Drives			
Modem			
VDU			
Printer			
Speakers			
Software			
Justification			

	Trevor (an accountant) and his staff are moving to offices in a brand-new building. Clients will send accounts on disk.	Jake is disabled and house-bound. Physical movement is limited. Jake wants a computer to help him improve his life style.	My ideal computer would be . . .
Casing			
Keyboard			
Mouse			
Rollerball			
Scanner			
Microphone			
Digital camera			
Hard disk			
RAM			
Processor			
Drives			
Modem			
VDU			
Printer			
Speakers			
Software			
Justification			

Activity 3.3

Formatted to insert 6 pt line space	

If you want to insert a table similar to the one illustrated above how many steps do you think it will take to achieve the same result? Seven? Nine? Ten? It is actually as many as 25 (or about 22 if you use some of the shortcuts that are available).

Long route

1 Select the Table Menu
2 Insert table
3 No. of columns – 2
4 No. of rows – 3
5 OK
6 Pause recording
7 Select the table
8 Resume recorder
9 Click Format
10 Borders & Shading
11 Choose the double outside line
12 Choose the grid
13 Click OK
14 Pause recording
15 Select the top row of the table
16 Resume recorder
17 Select font size 11 pt
18 Select font style Arial
19 Format to bold
20 Select Format
21 Paragraph
22 Set Line Spacing Before to 6 pt
23 Set Line Spacing After to 6 pt
24 OK
25 Stop recording

Using shortcuts

1 Click the Table icon
2 highlight the number of rows and columns
3 pause recording
4 Select the table
5 Resume recorder
6 Open the Borders toolbar by clicking the icon
7 Select a double line
8 Click on the Border button
9 Select single line
10 Click the Grid button
11 Pause recording
12 Select the top row of the table
13 Resume recorder
14 Select font size 11 pt
15 Select font style Arial
16 Format to bold
17 Select Format
18 Paragraph
19 Set Line Spacing Before to 6 pt
20 Set Line Spacing After to 6 pt
21 OK
22 Stop recording

This would make an excellent Macro! Two keystrokes and the table is inserted. Try it for yourself!

- create a macro to repeat the steps above
- test the macro
- print the macro coding
- edit the macro coding to change the table to 3 columns and 5 rows
- test the macro
- print the revised macro code
- annotate the revised code to show the changes you made.

Do you think it saves time?

If you were creating the macro for somebody else, you would need to produce user instructions so he or she could use the macro if you were not there to show him or her.

- Produce clear user instructions and print a copy.
- Close your computer system down.
- Hand your user instructions to a friend and ask him or her to use your macro.

Was he or she successful? Yes? Well done! Your user instructions were clear.

Was he or she successful? No? Take another look at your user instructions and edit as necessary.

Activity 3.4

You will have seen from the textbook on page 131 that, amongst their many uses, templates provide the way to store a frequently used document style in a form that can be used time and time again.

One activity you will repeat many times during the next few months is handing in your assessments. Your portfolio will look very professional if all your assessment front covers follow a consistent style of presentation.

Wouldn't it be helpful if you designed a front cover and stored it as a template?

Your template should include your name, course details, a position for the assessment title to be inserted, the mandatory/optional unit number and date. (If you use Insert/Date and Time the current date will automatically appear each time you open the template.) You might like also to illustrate the front cover with a graphic image.

We have shown two examples below:

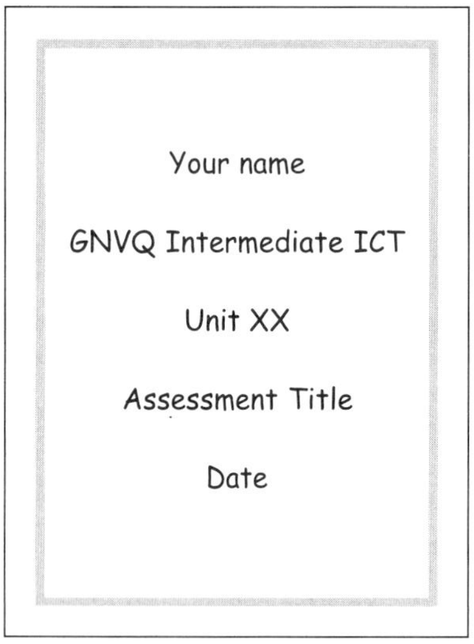

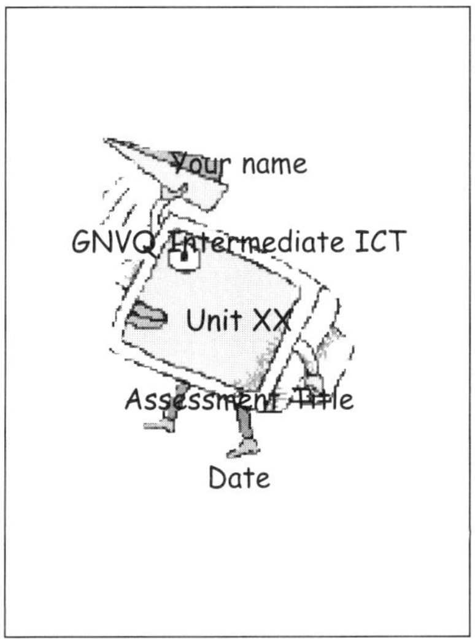

- Sketch your initial ideas by hand and annotate your designs to describe the font size/style and position you will use, images (position/size) you wish to include and the filename/path you will give to the front cover. The notes you make should mean someone else can produce the template exactly as you intended.
- Produce your front cover and save it as a template.
- Hand your description to a friend and ask him or her to produce the template from your notes. (Do the same for your friend, by the way!) If it matches the sketch design, you have produced a clear, detailed description. If it doesn't, look again at your description, see where your notes were unclear, cross through the original and change it.
- Test your template. Open it and insert the title **Practice Material** and **Unit 3**. Save the new document with a suitable filename.
- Provide a screen dump as evidence you have saved the template and the document.
- Produce brief user instructions so that a friend could find and use the template if you were not there to show him or her.
- Close the application in which you produced the template, hand your user instructions to your friend and ask him or her to find and use your template. If he or she managed to do this it shows your instructions were clear. If not, look at them again to see what needs inserting/editing.

Activity 3.5

If you buy a new computer you will have to set it up before you can use it. The right-hand column lists everything you will have to do but unfortunately it is in the wrong order.

Indicate the right order by joining the numbers on the left with the action that corresponds to it. The first one has been done for you. Now key in the list in the right order.

1	Instal print drivers and applications software if necessary
2	Health and safety – check cables are safely tucked away
3	If system doesn't power up check cables are plugged in
4	Power system up again
5	Open each application in turn
6	Exit the application for a second time
7	Carefully unpack each item of hardware from the box
8	Check and adjust monitor brightness control if necessary
9	Reopen each application; open the file and print
10	Turn power off and connect any remaining peripherals
11	Type in some test data and save
12	Create folders/directories as required
13	Connect cables for keyboard, mouse, VDU
14	Carry out system configuration
15	If system doesn't power up check cables are plugged in
16	Plug into main electricity supply to make sure system powers up
17	Close the application down after entering test data

Activity 3.5 – NOTES TO TUTORS

The left-hand column shows the item that goes with each number. The table below has been sorted in the order intended. Numbers 4 and 8 can be matched to either 3 or 15.

1/7	Instal print drivers and applications software if necessary
2/13	Health and safety – check cables are safely tucked away
3/16	If system doesn't power up check cables are plugged in
4/3 or 15	Power system up again
5/1	Open each application in turn
6/10	Exit the application for a second time
7/4	Carefully unpack each item of hardware from the box
8/15 or 3	Check and adjust monitor brightness control if necessary
9/8	Reopen each application; open the file and print
10/5	Turn power off and connect any remaining peripherals
11/11	Type in some test data and save
12/17	Create folders/directories as required
13/9	Connect cables for keyboard, mouse, VDU
14/6	Carry out system configuration
15/2	If system doesn't power up check cables are plugged in
16/12	Plug into main electricity supply to make sure system powers up
17/14	Close the application down after entering test data

7	Carefully unpack each item of hardware from the box
13	Connect cables for keyboard, mouse, VDU
16	Plug into main electricity supply to make sure system powers up
3 (or 15)	If system doesn't power up check cables are plugged in
1	Install print drivers and applications software if necessary
10	Turn power off and connect any remaining peripherals
4	Power system up again
15 (or 3)	If system doesn't power up check cables are plugged in
8	Check and adjust monitor brightness control if necessary
5	Open each application in turn
11	Type in some test data and save
17	Close the application down after entering test data
9	Reopen each application, open the test files and print
6	Exit the application for a second time
2	Health and safety – check cables are safely tucked away
12	Create folders/directories as required
14	Carry out system configuration

Activity 3.6

The illustration below shows the Control Panel on my computer:

Compare your Control Panel with the illustration above. Circle any icons you also have on your computer system and strike through those you do not have. List any additional icons below:

____

____

____

Why do you think there might be differences?

____

____

My computer is part of a network and some things I have access to and some I do not. For example, if I try to open  I get the following message on my screen!

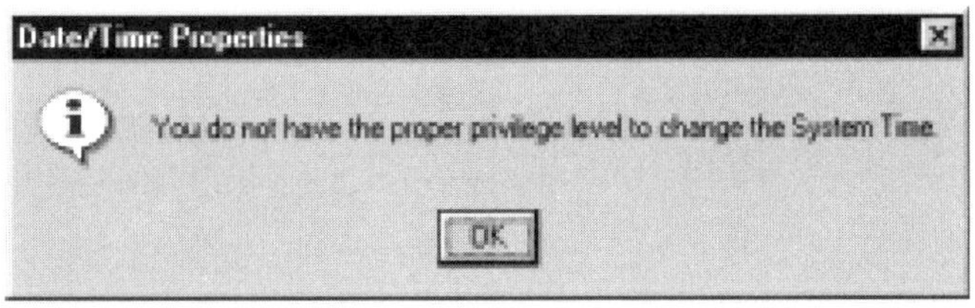

Why do you think this happens?

____

____

When I double-click  I gain access to Display Properties where I can, for example, change the desktop area to make the font size larger or smaller, or change the screensaver.

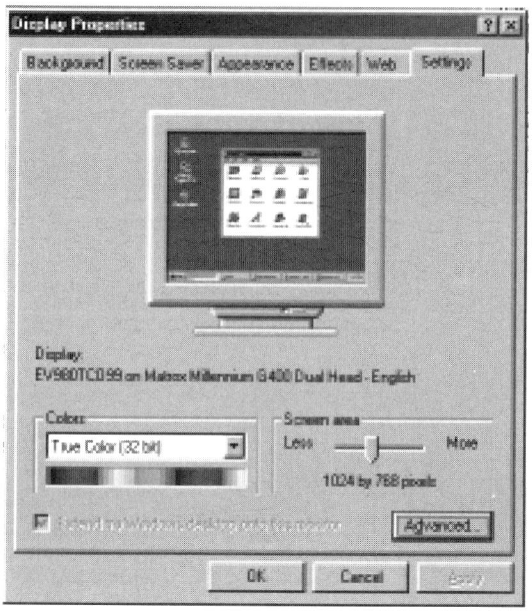

Do the changes I make affect the configuration of the applications or operating system software?

____

____

____

____

____

We have started a table to illustrate the configuration icons available on your system. Create a similar table, access the dialogue boxes and list the configuration settings you are able to change in each one, or note if you were unable to gain access.

Configuration icon	Configuration settings
	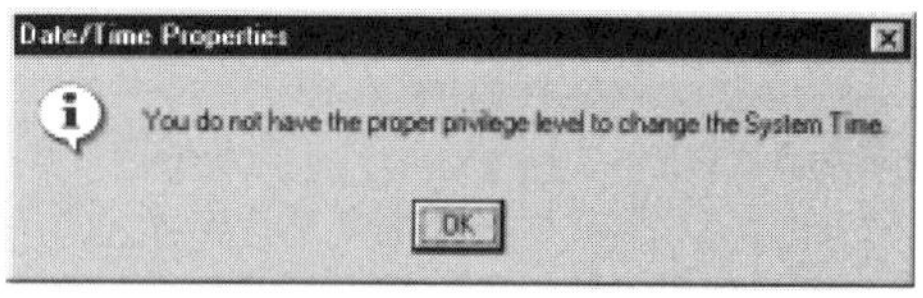 Unable to gain access to this dialogue
	Background – pattern and wallpaper Screensaver – e.g. flying objects, 3D pipes Appearance – e.g. colour Plus – change icons Settings – e.g. desktop area, refresh rate
	Speed – character repeat rate, cursor blink rate

Make a list of anything you don't know or don't understand below. When you have a class discussion about this activity you will be able to raise your questions and write in the answers.

What I don't understand	What it means

Activity 3.7

The following table has examples of dialogue boxes that enable a computer user to configure applications software. In the cell to the right of each illustration write down:

- The steps you take to access the dialogue box (e.g. Tools/Language/Set Language).
- The change to the applications software that might result from your actions.

Don't worry if you don't know everything. When you have a class discussion about this activity you will be able to write in the answers you didn't know.

<table>
<tr><td>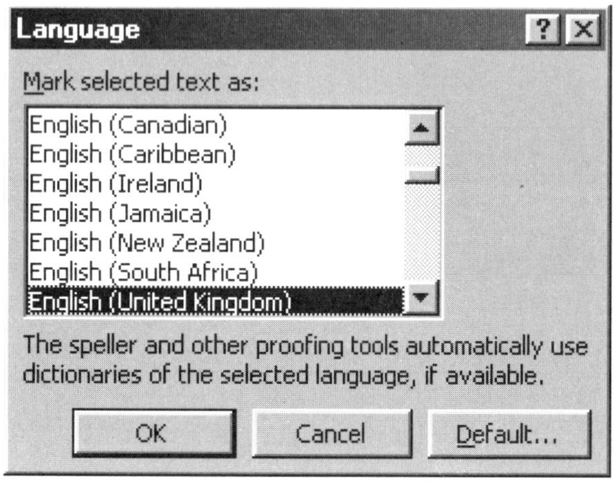
</td><td></td></tr>
<tr><td>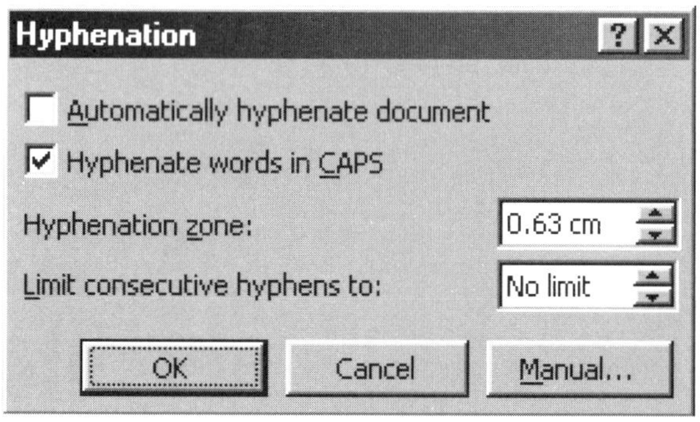
</td><td></td></tr>
<tr><td>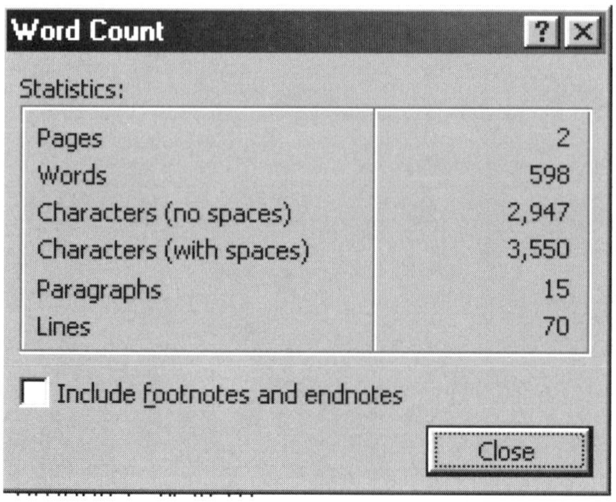
</td><td></td></tr>
</table>

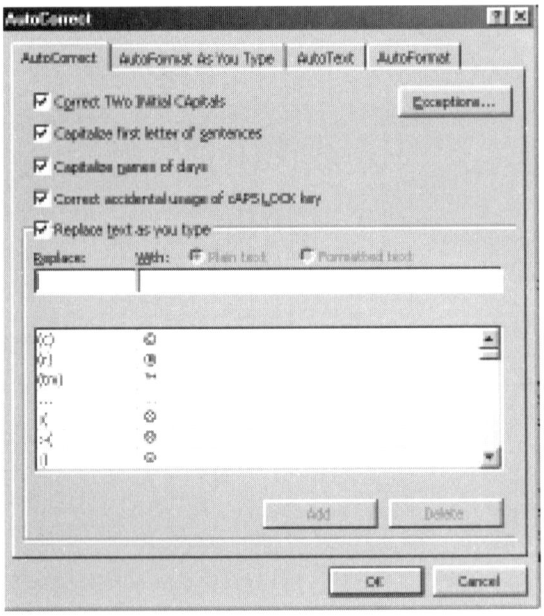 AutoCorrect AutoCorrect AutoFormat As You Type AutoText AutoFormat Correct TWo INitial CApitals Exceptions... Capitalize first letter of sentences Capitalize names of days Correct accidental usage of cAPS LOCK key Replace text as you type Replace: With: Plain text Formatted text Add Delete OK Cancel	
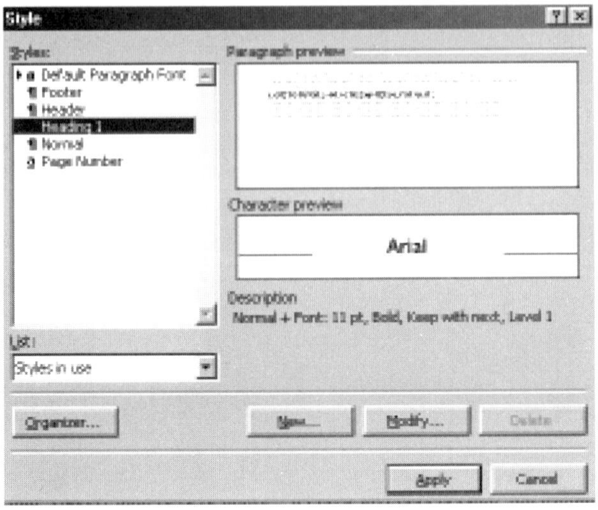 Style Styles: Default Paragraph Font Footer Header Heading 1 Normal Page Number Paragraph preview Character preview Arial Description Normal + Font: 11 pt, Bold, Keep with next, Level 1 List: Styles in use Organizer... New... Modify... Delete Apply Cancel	
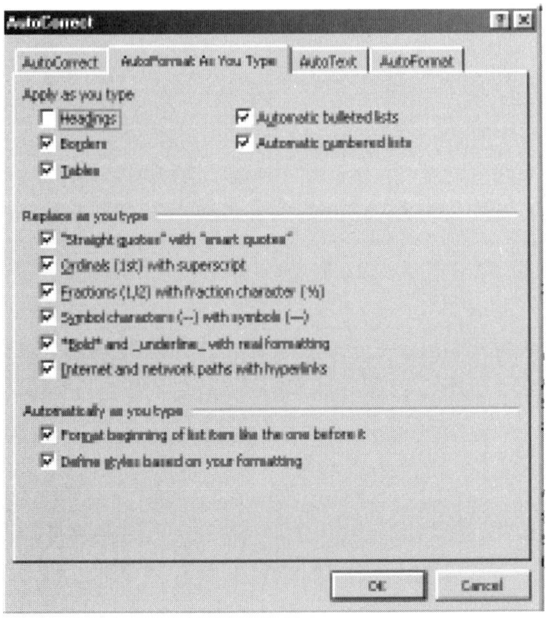 AutoCorrect AutoCorrect AutoFormat As You Type AutoText AutoFormat Apply as you type Headings Borders Tables Automatic bulleted lists Automatic numbered lists Replace as you type "Straight quotes" with "smart quotes" Ordinals (1st) with superscript Fractions (1/2) with fraction character (½) Symbol characters (--) with symbols (—) *Bold* and _underline_ with real formatting Internet and network paths with hyperlinks Automatically as you type Format beginning of list item like the one before it Define styles based on your formatting OK Cancel	

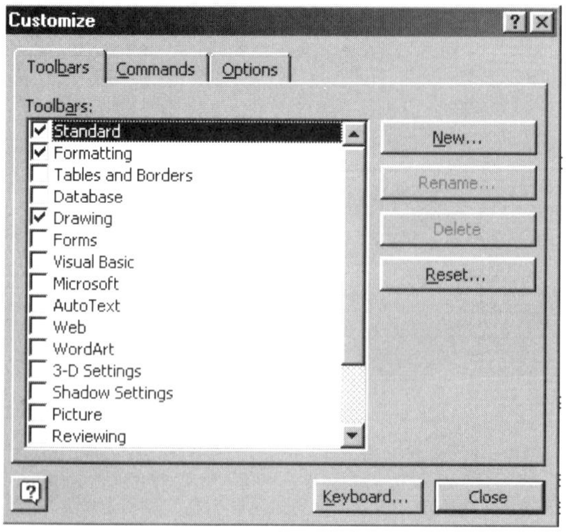
Customize
Toolbars
Commands
Options
Toolbars:
Standard
Formatting
Tables and Borders
Database
Drawing
Forms
Visual Basic
Microsoft
AutoText
Web
WordArt
3-D Settings
Shadow Settings
Picture
Reviewing
New...
Rename...
Delete
Reset...
Keyboard...
Close

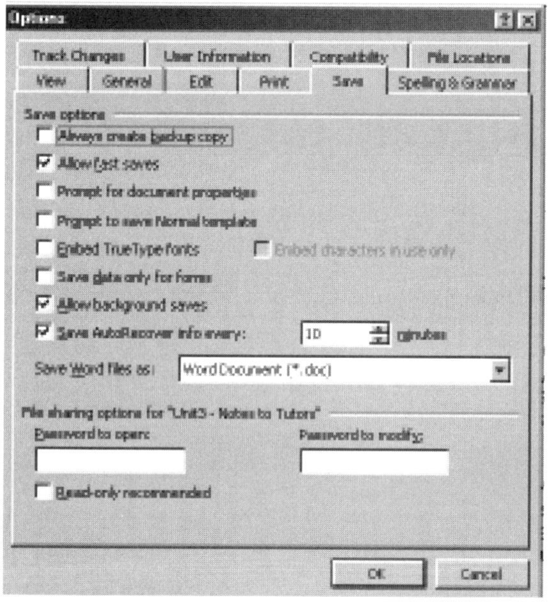
Options
Track Changes
User Information
Compatibility
File Locations
View
General
Edit
Print
Save
Spelling & Grammar
Save options
Always create backup copy
Allow fast saves
Prompt for document properties
Prompt to save Normal template
Embed TrueType fonts
Embed characters in use only
Save data only for forms
Allow background saves
Save AutoRecover info every:
10
minutes
Save Word files as:
Word Document (*.doc)
File sharing options for "Unit3 - Notes to Tutors"
Password to open:
Password to modify:
Read-only recommended
OK
Cancel

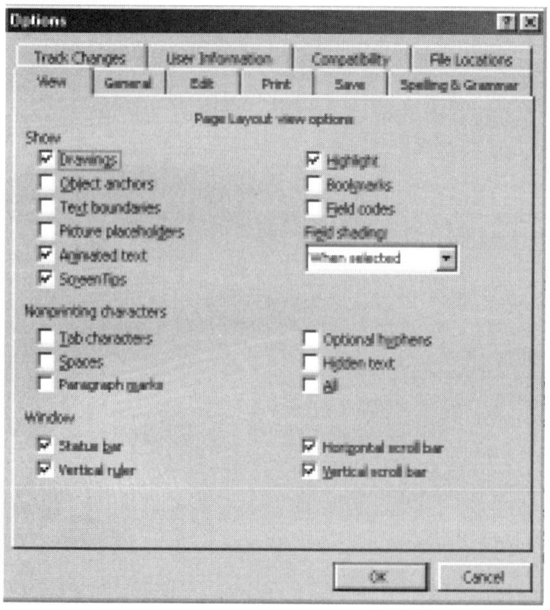
Options
Track Changes
User Information
Compatibility
File Locations
View
General
Edit
Print
Save
Spelling & Grammar
Page Layout view options
Show
Drawings
Object anchors
Text boundaries
Picture placeholders
Animated text
ScreenTips
Highlight
Bookmarks
Field codes
Field shading:
When selected
Nonprinting characters
Tab characters
Spaces
Paragraph marks
Optional hyphens
Hidden text
All
Window
Status bar
Vertical ruler
Horizontal scroll bar
Vertical scroll bar
OK
Cancel

Activity 3.8

The two screen dumps on the following page are from the top and bottom of a web site you are probably very familiar with – Microsoft Clip Gallery Live. The source code for this web page follows the screen dumps.

Look at the source code to see if you can find some of the basic html tags we looked at in the programming section in the textbook on page 140 (don't forget that some of them will have both opening and closing tags). For example:

- tags that indicate the beginning and end of an html page
- body tags
- heading tags
- paragraph tags
- comment tags
- anchor tags
- graphics files
- hyperlinks.

Indicate the type of tag in the first column of the table, highlight the tags in the code and number them to correspond with the number in the table.

We have done the first one for you.

1	*title tag*	`<title>Microsoft® Clip Gallery Live EULA</title>`
2		
3		
4		
5		
6		
7		
8		
9		
10		

Can you identify any of the text that appears on the web page amongst the source code? If so, highlight and number the text on the screen dump of the web page and also the corresponding code. See how much you are able to match.

Can you find any code that might indicate colour or font style?

What else can you find you think you might understand?

Microsoft® ClipGallery LIVE 2000

All Products | Support | Search | microsoft.com Guide

Microsoft

Home | License | Community | Feedback | Help |

ADDENDUM
to the MICROSOFT END USER LICENSE AGREEMENT
for
MICROSOFT OFFICE, MICROSOFT WORD, MICROSOFT EXCEL,
MICROSOFT POWERPOINT, MICROSOFT PUBLISHER,
MICROSOFT FRONTPAGE, MICROSOFT HOME PUBLISHING,
MICROSOFT PHOTODRAW, and MICROSOFT WORKS

By clicking the Accept button,
I signify that I have read and accept the terms below:

NOTE: Active scripting must be enabled in order to proceed.

Accept

This Addendum ("Addendum") is provided for the purpose of granting rights to licensed users of Microsoft Office, Microsoft Word, Microsoft Excel, Microsoft PowerPoint, Microsoft Publisher, Microsoft FrontPage, Microsoft Home Publishing, Microsoft PhotoDraw, and Microsoft Works (individually the "SOFTWARE PRODUCT") which are in addition to the rights set forth in the Microsoft End User License Agreement for the

Microsoft makes no representation or warranty as to the right of users to utilize any individual's name, likeness and/or image appearing in the CONTENT. Users may not commercially exploit any individual's name, likeness, and/or image WITHOUT first obtaining the appropriate rights of publicity license directly from each individual.

TRADEMARK/LOGO RIGHTS:

This CONTENT has not been cleared or approved for use as trademarks or logos in conjunction with any companies' products or services. Microsoft makes no representation or warranty as to the right of users to utilize the CONTENT in this manner. If you are considering use of the CONTENT for this purpose, you should consult a competent attorney as use of some CONTENT could infringe trademark or other intellectual property rights of third parties. **BY USING THIS CONTENT, YOU AGREE NOT TO ASSERT ANY INTELLECTUAL PROPERTY RIGHTS, INCLUDING BUT NOT LIMITED TO CLAIMS OF TRADEMARK INFRINGEMENT, AGAINST MICROSOFT NOW OR IN THE FUTURE.**

▲ Back to the TOP to accept this EULA!

```
<!DOCTYPE HTML PUBLIC "-//W3C//DTD HTML 4.01 Frameset//EN">
<html>
  <head>
    <title>Microsoft® Clip Gallery Live EULA</title>          ①
    <meta http-equiv="Content-Type" content="text/html; charset=iso-8859-1">
    <meta name="GENERATOR" content="Microsoft FrontPage 4.0">
    <meta name="ProgId" content="FrontPage.Editor.Document">
    <link rel="stylesheet" type="text/css" href="cgl.css">
    <script language="javascript">
      var tUserAgent = "Mozilla/4.0 (compatible; MSIE 5.0; Windows NT; DigExt)"
      var tRemoteAddr = "195.194.61.10"
    </script>
    <script language="javascript" type="text/javascript"
src="cci_cgl.js"></script>
    <script language="javascript" type="text/javascript" src="cgl.js"></script>
      <!—TOOLBAR_EXEMPT—>

  </head>  <frameset rows="80,*" border="0" frameborder="0" frameborder="no"
framespacing="0">
    <frame name="toolbar" src="eulatoolbar.asp?nInterface=0" scrolling="no"
marginheight="0" marginwidth="0" noresize>
    <frame name="eula" src="eulaform.htm" scrolling="auto" marginheight="0"
marginwidth="0" noresize>
    <noframes>

  <body bgcolor="#FFFFFF" text="#000000" topmargin="0" leftmargin="0"
  marginwidth="0" marginheight="0">
    <table width="100%" cellpadding="0" cellspacing="0" border="0"
    bgcolor="#FFFFFF">
      <tr>
        <td valign="top" height="60" width="100%" rowspan="2"><img
          src="images/banner.gif" alt="Microsoft® Clip Gallery Live"
border="0"></td>
        <td valign="top" height="20" align="right"><img
          src="../../library/toolbar/images/curve.gif" alt border="0"
width="18"
          height="20"></td>
        <td bgcolor="#000000" height="20" valign="middle" align="right" nowrap
        colspan="2"><font face="Verdana, Arial, Helvetica" size="1"
          color="#FFFFFF"><b>  <a
          style="color:#FFFFFF;text-decoration:none;"
          href="/isapi/gomscom.asp?target=/products/" target="_top">All
Products</a>  |
            <a style="color:#FFFFFF;text-decoration:none;"
          href="/isapi/gomscom.asp?target=/support/"
target="_top">Support</a>  |
            <a style="color:#FFFFFF;text-decoration:none;"
          href="/isapi/gosearch.asp?target=/"
target="_top">Search</a>  |
            <a style="color:#FFFFFF;text-decoration:none;"
          href="/isapi/gomscom.asp?target=/" target="_top">microsoft.com
Home</a>  </b></font></td>
      </tr>
      <tr>
        <td valign="top" height="40" width="19"><img
          src="../../library/images/gifs/homepage/1ptrans.gif" alt border="0"
          width="1" height="1"></td>
        <td valign="top" height="40" align="right" nowrap colspan="2"><a
          href="/isapi/gomscom.asp?target=/" target="_top"><img
          src="../../library/toolbar/images/mslogo.gif" alt="Microsoft"
          border="0" width="112" height="40"></a></td>
```

```
      </tr>
      <tr>
        <td bgcolor="#0066CC" height="20" valign="middle" nowrap
colspan="4"> </td>
      </tr>
    </table>
    <blockquote>
      <p align="center"><font face="Verdana, Arial, Helvetica" size="2">A
        browser such as <a
        href="http://www.microsoft.com/windows/ie/download/default.asp"
        target="_top">Microsoft Internet Explorer 5</a> that supports scripting
        and frames is required for Clip Gallery Live. You must also be a
        licensed user of a product that includes the Microsoft Clip Gallery
3.0
        or greater, such as Microsoft Office, Microsoft Publisher, Microsoft
        FrontPage, or Microsoft Works to open the downloaded clips. Click <a
        href="http://www.microsoft.com/windows/ie/download/default.asp"
        target="_top">Get Microsoft Internet Explorer</a> to install the most
        current browser available today. Once installed, you can return to
take
        full advantage of all the exciting new pictures, sounds, and motion
        clips!</font></p>
    </blockquote>
    <p align="center"><font face="Verdana, Arial, Helvetica"
size="1"><nobr>©2000
      Microsoft Corporation.</nobr> <nobr>All rights reserved.</nobr> <nobr><a
      href="http://www.microsoft.com/info/cpyright.htm" target="_blank">Terms
of
      Use</a></nobr> <nobr><a href="http://www.microsoft.com/info/privacy.htm"
      target="_blank">Privacy Policy</a></nobr></font></p>
    <p> </p>
  </body>    </noframes>
  </frameset>
```

Activity 3.9

Open evening is coming and your tutor would like a web page produced to give new students and their families some information about your course and the students currently on it.

For this activity to be successful you need to work with two other students because the aim is to create a four-page web site – two pages created by you and one page each by your two friends.

Stage 1

Produce a simple web page, using Notepad or a wizard, to introduce the Intermediate Certificate in Information and Communications Technology in your school or college.

Your web page might indicate the days and times you are in college and describe the ICT facilities available to you. You could include an introduction to the units you are studying and write a short paragraph about yourself and what you particularly like about your course. (You should produce the equivalent to an A4 page.)

At the foot of the page use a suitable anchor tag to take you back up to the top of the page. (Look in your textbook on page 136 to remind yourself how to do this.)

Make sure you save the page in your web page folder. Test your page in a web browser to see if it looks as you intended and to check your hyperlink. Print the web page and the html code.

Stage 2

Produce a .gif file with an image of yourself – either scanned or taken with a digital camera. Do you remember why it should be a .gif file? If not, refer to your textbook, page 137.

Produce a second web page incorporating your picture and write a short paragraph about your hobbies and interests out of college. Add two further paragraphs describing briefly the two friends you are working with. (You will later use their names to create hyperlinks to the pages they are producing about themselves.)

Save this second page in your web page folder. View the page in your web browser, print a copy of the page and the coding.

Stage 3

Create a hyperlink between these two pages. Your aim is to add a sentence to the paragraph about yourself on the first page which reads 'If you want to find out more about me click here', so that when you click you jump to your second page.

Edit the html code in your first page to include the text above and a suitable destination anchor tag.

Test your web pages in the web browser and print a copy of the web page and the code.

Stage 4

Insert a hyperlink on your second page to take you back to your first page.

Test the hyperlink and print a copy of the web page and the revised html code.

Stage 5

In Stage 2 you and your friends each created a similar page about yourselves. The final aim of this activity is that you will now create hyperlinks to their pages by clicking on their names on your second page. They in turn will click on your name in their second page to open your page.

Your tutor will help you with this part of the activity. You may be able to save your personal pages in an area of your school or college network that is accessible to all students, or you may need to save copies of their html files in your own area.

Stage 6

When you have successfully managed to create the hyperlinks to your friends' pages you should think about the navigation through your pages and insert suitable hyperlinks to enable you to move from one page to another and back to your home page.

UNIT 5 PRACTICE – INFORMATION RESOURCES

PRACTICE PRE-RELEASE MATERIALS

Candidate brief

Read the following instructions carefully. They tell you what work you must do, what you must produce and what to bring along to the external test on this unit. In each case you must make a note of the precise reference material used and include this as a separate list with the rest of the work. Your notes on using paper-based resources and the list of sources used must be word processed. The work you are asked to produce will be marked along with your test and together these marks will give you a grade for the unit.

The work you do on the tasks should each have a title (e.g. Task 1, Task 2) and should include your name, your registration number, the unit name, the test date and your centre name and number.

You must bind these documents in the order they appear here.

Each of the six tasks will be marked out of 3 for the quality of the work you produce. The total, out of 18, will be added to your test score.

You are required to do the following six tasks.

Using ICT resources

Task 1

Use a CD-ROM to extract and print one page of information (containing both text and images) about the Great White Shark. You must note the name of the CD you have used and the type of information (encyclopaedia, history, science, etc.) it contains.

Task 2

Use the Internet to download, extract, edit and print two pages of information about the work of psychiatrist Carl Gustav Jung. The extract should contain both images and text and should concentrate on his work (rather than his life). Note the Internet addresses of the information you have used.

Task 3

Use the Internet to extract, edit and print a page of information about the world's 20 richest people. The information should contain a table, chart or other relevant image. Keep a note of the name of the information supplier and the web-sites involved.

Using paper-based resources

Note: The notes produced in the paper-based tasks should be brief and in your own words. They must not be word-for-word copies of existing material. If you do use small quotations from existing material you should make it clear it is a quotation.

Task 4

Go to a library and use an encyclopaedia or similar reference book to look up what information you can about Sir Christopher Wren. Word process a one-page summary of information about him and his work. Your summary must contain two small illustrations, each no larger than 4 cm × 4 cm, suitably positioned and relevant to the subject. These might be scanned or downloaded from the Internet. Also make a note of the name of the book you have used for your research together with the volume (if more than one), chapter, page, editor, publisher and date of publication.

Task 5

Use a travel book or magazine to look up information about the city of Vancouver. Produce a one-page word processed summary about:

- The city's position in Canada.
- Totem poles.

You must include two illustrations (each not greater than 4 cm × 4 cm) which are suitably positioned and are relevant to the subject.

Note the name of the book or magazine you have used, by whom it was published, its editor, date of publication and page numbers of references used.

Task 6

Use a newspaper to look up yesterday's maximum temperature, hours of sunshine and inches of rainfall for the following places:

- London
- Edinburgh
- Cardiff
- Belfast.

Make a note of the newspaper used and the date you looked up the information.

You will need to hand in, together with your test paper:

- One page extracted and printed from a CD for Task 1.
- Two pages extracted and printed using the Internet for Task 2.
- One page printed from the Internet for Task 3.
- Word processed notes (not more than one page) for Task 4.
- Word processed notes (not more than one page) for Task 5.
- A word processed note of the temperatures, annual rainfall and sunshine for Task 6.
- A list of sources used as specified in the tasks and related to the relevant task.

Practice external test – Unit 5

Start time: .... Test length: $1\frac{1}{2}$ hours

Total marks: 100

Centre no.
Registration no.
Centre name
Last name and initials

FOR EXAMINER USE ONLY

TOTAL MARKS

Total	

Instructions to Candidates

In the boxes above, write your centre number and registration number, the centre name and your last name and initials.

Answer ALL questions, using the spaces provided. If you need additional space, you should continue your answers at the end, indicating clearly which question you are answering.

1 You visited a library to find out about Sir Christopher Wren.

a Briefly describe how you used the catalogue to find a book.

3 marks

b Briefly describe how you located the book in the library.

2 marks

c Give the title and reference number of a book you used.

3 marks

(Total **8** marks)

2 Suppose that when finding information about Vancouver you learnt there is a chapter on totem poles in a book called *Coastal Tribes of the North West Pacific*.

Describe the steps you could take to locate this chapter and obtain a copy for your use at home.

(Total 9 marks)

3 When working on the pre-release material, you had to use information from paper sources and from ICT sources.

Choose one ICT source (CD-ROM or the Internet) and one paper-based source (reference book, magazine or newspaper) and say which you found easiest to use and why.

(Total 9 marks)

4 When trying to find information you may have to contact an organisation directly. To make your search more efficient, you need to begin with the department that most often deals with that type of information.

For each of the departments below, give two examples of the types of information they deal with.

Sales

a

b

IT services

a

b

Human resources

a

b

(Total 12 marks)

5 When you were working on the pre-release material you had to proofread your work to ensure accuracy and readability.

Briefly describe how you did this.

(Total 9 marks)

6 Nowadays, it can be really difficult to find good quality (accurate, up-to-date and concise) information. This is because there is lots of information that is often irrelevant to your search.

Explain what you understand by the term 'information overload' and briefly describe three techniques that can be used to manage information.

(Total 9 marks)

7 All organisations have to comply with the principles of the Data Protection Act when storing the information they gather and use.

Briefly describe two ways companies manage information within the Act.

(Total 8 marks)

8 There are several ICT methods by which organisations communicate information internally. Briefly describe three methods, their advantages and their disadvantages.

(Total 9 marks)

9 Using the Internet to conduct searches can result in thousands of irrelevant links. Briefly explain three search tips that you would recommend when using search tools.

(Total 9 marks)

(Total marks for Unit 5: 100)

Test mark scheme

Where 2 or 3 marks are given for any single point made, the second and third marks should generally be used to reflect the higher skills required for Merit and Distinction grades.

1 You visited a library to find out about Sir Christopher Wren.

a Briefly describe how you used the catalogue to find a book.
Brief description of use of catalogue. — *3 marks*

b Briefly describe how you located the book in the library.
Location by category. — *1 mark*
Use of Dewey number. — *1 marks*

c Give the title and reference number of a book you used.
Title and reference given. — *1 mark for title*
2 marks for reference
(Total 8 marks)

2 Suppose that when finding information about Vancouver, you learnt there is a chapter on totem poles in a book called *Coastal Tribes of the North West Pacific.*

Describe the steps you could take to locate this chapter and obtain a copy for your use at home.

Three of: author, title, date, keywords or similar. — *1 mark each (total 3)*
Two of library, the Internet, a book of abstracts, (travel agent?). — *2 marks*
Narrative of either look-up or method (photocopy, edit CD, etc.). — *4 marks*
(Total 9 marks)

3 When working on the pre-release material you had to use information from paper sources and from ICT sources.

Choose one ICT source (CD-ROM or the Internet) and one paper-based source (reference book, magazine or newspaper) and say which you found easiest to use and why.

This question allows candidates to exhibit higher-grade skills such as fluency, understanding, accuracy, planning, etc.

Short essay bringing out a balance between paper and ICT, including:

<u>ICT</u>
Information in a small space
Information fast to access and manipulate
Good indexing
Data can be manipulated.

<u>Paper</u>
Often more portable
No power source needed
Often cheaper.
(Total 9 marks)

4 When trying to find information, you may have to contact an organisation directly. To make your search more efficient, you need to begin with the department that most often deals with that type of information.

For each of the departments below, give two examples of the types of information they deal with.

Give 2 marks for each point:

<u>Sales</u>
Provide information to customers, demonstrate products, advise customers on their choices, exchange goods for money, credit or debit cards, provide receipts, other relevant points. — *4 marks*

IT services
Computer and peripheral purchases, maintenance, repairs, modifications, LAN installation and connections, user support, other relevant points. *4 marks*
Human resources
Drawing up job descriptions, contracts, interview procedures, advertising for staff, pay and benefits processing, organisational training and development, other relevant points. *4 marks*
(Total 12 marks)

5 When you were working on the pre-release material you had to proofread your work to ensure accuracy and readability.

Briefly describe how you did this.

Give 3 marks for each point from:
Spell checking
Grammar checking
Readability statistic checking
Use of basic proofreading symbols
Avoiding technical language
Explaining acronyms
Checking level of formality
Other relevant points. *(Total 9 marks)*

6 Nowadays, it can be really difficult to find good-quality (accurate, up-to-date and concise) information. This is because there is so much information that is often irrelevant to your search.

Explain what you understand by the term 'information overload' and briefly describe three techniques that can be used to manage information.

Paragraph focusing on the many sources of information and individuals (and/or organisations) becoming overwhelmed. *3 marks*

Prioritising
Rejecting irrelevancies
Not delaying dealing with information
Making efficient use of telephone
Not giving out e-mail address
Scanning e-mail headers for relevance
Using effective search techniques
Exploiting library facilities
Other relevant points. *6 marks*
(Total 9 marks)

7 All organisations have to comply with the principles of the Data Protection Act when storing the information they gather and use.

Briefly describe two ways companies manage information within the Act.

This is another question that allows candidates to exhibit higher-grade skills such as fluency, understanding, accuracy, planning, etc.

Candidates' comments might include:

Private information
Disclosure
Individual rights
Differences between paper and ICT-based storage
Company lawyers, law departments
Individuals specifically trained
Login codes, passwords, access rights/privileges, etc. *(Total 8 marks)*

8 There are several ICT methods by which organisations communicate information internally. Briefly describe three methods, their advantages and their disadvantages.

This question also allows candidates to exhibit higher-grade skills such as fluency, understanding, accuracy, planning, etc.

NB: Where 3 marks are given for any single point made, the second and third marks should generally be used to reflect the higher skills required for Merit and Distinction grades.

Candidates should describe any of the following:

Telephone
E-mail
Intranet
Memorandum.

(Total 9 marks)

9 Using the Internet to conduct searches can result in thousands of irrelevant links. Briefly explain three search tips that you would recommend when using search tools.

Candidates should comment on any of the following:

Using lower case

Using quotation marks
Asking direct questions
Using operators
Other relevant points.

(Total 9 marks)

Marking the pre-release tasks

Each of the six tasks will be marked out of three using the following criteria:

0 – Work which is worthless.
1 – Work which contains a little detail.
2 – Good work with some missing details.
3 – Excellent work with little or no missing details.

The total, out of 18, to be added to the test score.

(Total 18 marks)

(Total marks for Unit 5: 100)

Question	Pass	Merit	Distinction	Total
1a	1	1	1	3
1b	1	1		2
1c	1	1	1	3
2	4	3	2	9
3	4	3	2	9
4	6	4	2	12
5	4	3	2	9
6	5	2	2	9
7	4	2	2	8
8	3	3	3	9
9	4	3	2	9
Tasks	9	5	4	18
Totals	46	31	23	100

UNIT 6 PRACTICE – GRAPHICS

NOTES TO TUTORS

We have included a selection of activities that give students the opportunity to practise all the graphics skills required for this unit.

Activity 6.1 (Fam_Tree-Activity.doc) suggests an activity for designing a family tree.

Activity 6.2 (bedroom.doc) gives practice in drawing to scale. This activity could be done using a simple drawing package or specialised interior design software.

Activity 6.3 (swing seat.doc) asks students to produce an instruction leaflet to assemble a garden swing using bitmap and vector drawing packages.

Activity 6.4 (Ferdi and garden.doc) is another example of drawing to scale. As with Activity 6.2 this could also be done using a simple drawing package or specialised garden design software.

Activity 6.5 (new logo.doc) provides an opportunity for imaginative design as well as practising duplicating and cloning techniques.

Activity 6.6 (Image Stitch.doc) – a selection of photographs has been provided for students to practise image stitching using smudging and smearing to blend the join. The images are saved as photos 1, 1A, 2, 2A, 3 and 3A.

Activity 6.1

A family tree is often used to show how family members are related to each other. The example below shows how the Princes William and Harry are related to their grandparents, aunts, uncles and cousins:

The Royal Family Tree

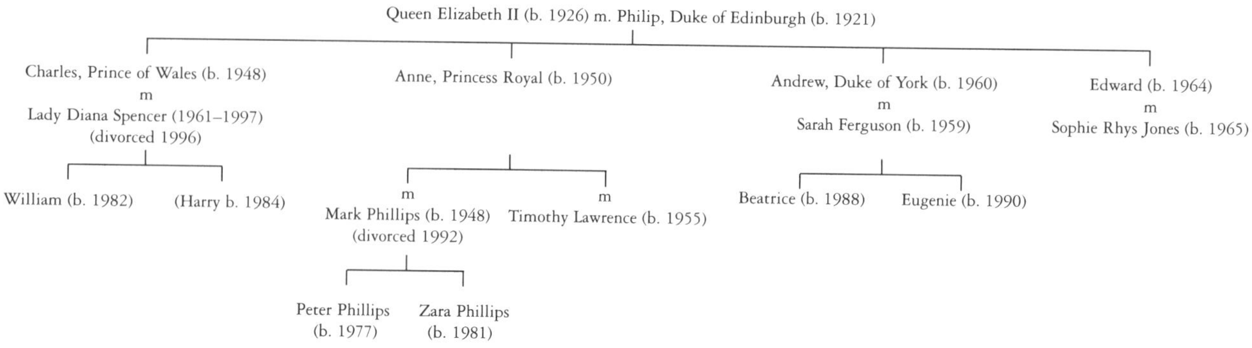

See if you can produce your own family tree showing your grandparents, parents and brothers and sisters or other relatives.

Save.

Print.

Activity 6.2

Choose a suitable graphics application that will let you produce scaled drawings.

Task 1

When you get home tonight draw a sketch plan of your bedroom.

Measure the room and write the dimensions on the sketch plan.

Show the position of your bedroom furniture on the plan.

Task 2

At school or college produce a scaled image of your bedroom.

Show the dimensions on the plan.

Print a copy of the image.

Annotate the print to identify the different tools/techniques you used to produce the plan.

Task 3

Remove the dimensions from your plan.

Place your furniture in the room to reflect your sketch plan.

Label the furniture.

Print two copies of the new room plan.

On one copy annotate the print to identify the different tools/techniques you used.

Task 4

We would like you to imagine your bedroom is completely empty – no furniture . . . no mess – and you suddenly find yourself with lots of spare cash!! At last you have the opportunity to completely redesign your room and to get yourself sorted out.

Re-plan your ideal room and label the furniture.

Print a copy.

Now all you have to do is dream!

Activity 6.3

We recently bought a self-assembly kit to put together a small child's tricycle and found the following diagram in the box to help us to do it:

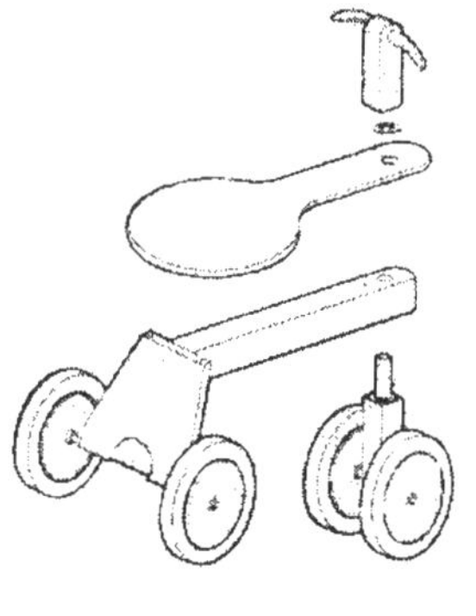

The diagram clearly shows how all the components fit together.

A friend is planning to sell garden swings in kit form comprising a drilled wooden seat, two looped ropes and two large screw-in hooks from which to suspend the swing. You can see the components illustrated below:

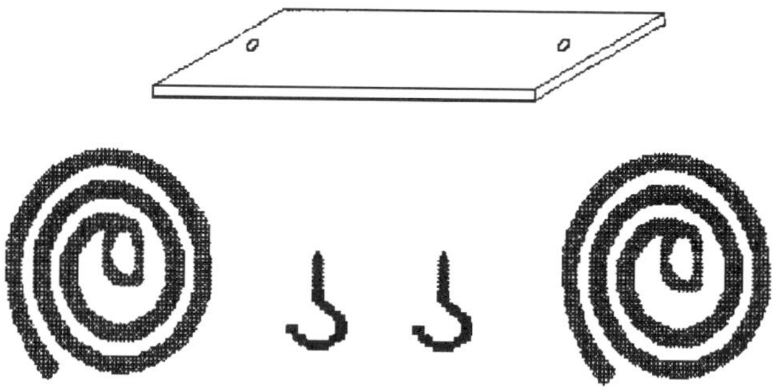

The hooks are intended to screw into a wooden frame, the ropes will loop over the hooks, pass down through the seat and tie with large knots under the seat.

Task 1

You have been asked to produce the leaflet to go in the swing pack showing the assembly instructions. Your leaflet should include graphic images showing the components separately (similar to above) and another to illustrate the assembly process (similar to the tricycle illustration).

Task 2

You will also need to add a written description.

(It might help you to know that to produce the illustration above we used both bitmap and vector drawing packages and the hook is a ? flipped in a bitmap package and edited pixel by pixel to resemble a screw fitting.)

Save.

Print.

Activity 6.4

Ferdi and his partner, Jif, have just bought a new house. The front garden has been grassed over but the back garden is just mud.

The back garden is rectangular, measuring 30 m long × 15 m wide and, although they have some ideas for the garden design, they can't visualise how their ideas will work out.

Ferdi would like a patio between his house and the start of the lawn. It should be large enough to accommodate an oval table and four chairs plus a barbecue so that they can entertain in the garden during the summer.

Jif wants a garden path so that she can walk in the garden when it is wet without getting her feet muddy. Ferdi wants some flowerbeds.

Ferdi would like a shed at the end of the garden. Sheds come in a variety of sizes from small to large – 2 m × 1 m, 1.5 m × 1.5 m, 2 m × 1.5 m, 3 m × 2 m.

Jif wants a summerhouse as far away from the house as possible so she can sit in the garden and get away from the television and telephone. Her favourite is round. They too come in different sizes with diameters of 2 m, 2.5 m or 3 m. She doesn't want to see the shed from the summerhouse door but would like to look over the flowerbeds.

Ferdi and Jif need to know if their garden is big enough to let them do what they have been imagining.

Task 1

Produce two garden plans to help them make their decision.

Task 2

Save.

Print.

Activity 6.5

Your school or college's marketing department has come up with a bright idea to represent all the courses on offer with a logo.

You are going to produce the logo for the GNVQ Intermediate Certificate in Information and Communication Technology.

Your design brief is that it should have an image reflecting the course content and it should include the initials GNVQ and ICT.

Task 1

Sketch out three designs and then try to recreate them using both bitmap and vector graphics software.

Save.

Print.

Task 2

Produce printouts of your logos at *each* stage of production and annotate them to indicate the tools/techniques you have tried. Make a note to indicate which techniques were more successful than others. You will find it useful to refer to these notes when you complete your graphics assessment.

Task 3

If you have suitable software available, experiment by *duplicating* your image to make a pattern incorporating at least ten similar images.

Print a copy of the pattern.

Edit your original image and see what happens to the other nine images.

Print another copy of the pattern and annotate it to identify the changes you have made.

Task 4

Now *clone* your original image and make a similar pattern incorporating at least ten similar images.

Print a copy of the pattern.

Edit the original image again and see what happens to the other nine images.

Experiment with various tools/techniques (e.g. smudging/smearing).

Print copies of the pattern at each stage and annotate it to remind yourself of the tools/techniques you used.

Task 5

When you have finished make a list of the successful techniques and also a list of the techniques you did not like.

Say what you did not like about them.

Save.

Print.

Activity 6.6

A selection of photographs is available in this tutors resource file (see Appendix 3), where two photographs have been taken of one view in order to include the whole scene.

Select a pair of your choice and try to stitch the images together. You may find it helpful to use smudging or smearing techniques where the images join.

Save.

Print.

UNITS 2 & 10 (COMBINED) PRACTICE – HANDLING INFORMATION & DATABASE TECHNIQUES AND APPLICATIONS

NOTES TO TUTORS

Before issuing this practice activity (saved as 3Ls_dBaseU10.doc), you may find it helpful to look at the rationale behind Assessment 10.1, as the tasks are designed to follow the same pattern. As with the actual assessment material, the requirements for this database have been kept as simple as possible, whilst still addressing the guidelines in the GNVQ standards. Although Unit 10 does require students to create three related tables, in our view, for the purpose of practice, two will be sufficient. Only a small sample of data has been included, since the purpose is to learn how to design, implement and search the database rather than enter data. This data is on page 42. A model of the database is included in the CD-ROM (saved as Loose Limbs_U10.mdb.

Activity 10.1 has been divided into five stages. In our experience students may be overwhelmed by a huge assessment, and also they do prefer to get on with creating a database, ignoring the planning stages. Therefore it may be advantageous to issue the five stages separately. The stages are as follows:

- *Part A: design.* Forms for this have been included in Appendix 2.
- *Part B: implementation.* A field for 'gender' has been included in the worked example. The students will probably not include this field, as it is not obvious from the data provided. This is deliberate so that when they reach Task 10, which requires a list of lady members, they will have to amend their database design.
- *Part C: testing.* After deleting the test data, students will find the autocounter will not start at number 1. They can either allow the autocounter to continue, or delete the primary key for members and then reinstate it.
- *Part D: entering/saving data and searching for information.* The reports required for Tasks 7, 8 and 9 are included in the worked example, but not Tasks 10 and 11 as these reports necessitate changes to the original file:
  - Task 10 – to make this search the students will have to delete a record and probably amend the design of the database and include a male/female field.
  - Task 11 – to make this search the two records will need to be edited.
- *Part E – evaluating the database.*

Activity 10.1

Scenario

The 3L's Club (Loose Limbs Leisure) has recently installed a computer system and has approached ICT Solutions Ltd to design a database to keep track of members' details and trainers' details. You have been given the task of planning, designing and implementing a suitable relational database. Currently the details are written in a card index system and include the following information:

Members' details

Membership number, title, last name, first name, address (street), town, post code, telephone number, date of birth. Also included is whether they use a private trainer and if so the trainer's ID.

Trainers' details

Trainer's ID, title, last name, first name, telephone number, category, hourly rate.

Part A: design

Task 1

Following the guidelines on pages 223–224 in your textbook, produce suitable entity relationship diagrams for two related tables, 'Members' and 'Trainers'.

Use the two copies of Form A to plan the design of a suitable database file for these two related tables.

Look back to the section on 'Setting up a computerised database' in Unit 2 on page 74. Think carefully about the following:

- The primary key for each table. (The members need a unique membership number, which may be created as a field with a *sequenced counter*, so each new member is automatically given the next number in the sequence. The trainers also need a unique ID which is based on a three-digit code using their initials.)
- How these two tables can be linked together.
- Any other fields that may be useful.
- The length and type of field – consider carefully the best way to design the fields.
- Which of those fields would be secondary keys (indexed).
- Whether you could use a range check.
- Whether a field should be required or not.

Using Form B, explain in one or two sentences why you have chosen each different type of field. For example, if several fields are text fields, you can give *one* explanation for choosing text for all the text fields.

Part B: implementation

Task 2

Make sure you have created a directory/folder for Unit 10 and subdirectory/folder called **Practice** and save all your work for this activity in the Practice directory/folder using a *suitable* filename.

Having planned the design of your database, you should now create the two tables using the database software.

Build the relationship between the two tables.

Print the relationship form.

Print the design details for both tables.

Note: If you are using Microsoft Access 97, to print the table design requested, select the **Tables** tab 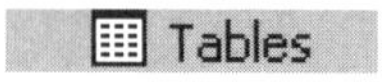

and from the **Tools** menu, choose:

Analyzer, Documenter, Options and then select the boxes illustrated

(For Access version 2, select **File, Add-ins, Database Documenter**).

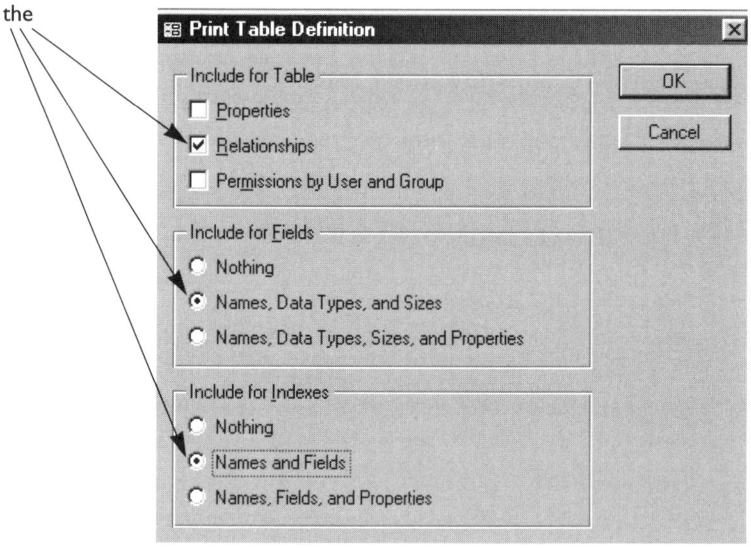

Task 3

From the tables, create the **Form** view.

If the software you are using is suitable, enhance the form design as you feel fit (e.g. use suitable fonts, point size, a heading, colour, shading). The form design should *not* occupy more than one screen page.

Print a copy of the form for both tables.

Save the file.

Task 4

To make your database more user-friendly to the non-technical person, design:

- An opening screen with buttons to access the different sections of the database.
- Buttons to toggle between the forms and the opening screen.
- A button to exit the database.

Print a copy of the form for the two tables and also the opening form.

Annotate the printouts to explain the benefits to users.

Demonstrate the buttons to your tutor.

Part C: testing

Task 5

Refer to the section 'Testing' in Unit 10 on page 233 in your textbook.

Create a log of testing for both tables using the following headings:

Field Name	Field Type	Data to Enter	Expected Result	Actual Result

You *must* use your own data for this purpose, *not the data provided.*

Don't forget to test for data which you expect to be rejected (e.g. text in a number field).

Enter your test data *as shown in the test log* into the database.

Print relevant reports from the testing.

Annotate the printouts noting any problems you encounter. If necessary correct the design of the tables, explaining why you have made the changes.

Once you are satisfied with your testing, make a backup copy of your file.

Print screen dumps showing the file saved on the hard drive and the floppy disk.

Make a third copy of the database, giving it a *new name*. Delete all test records from this file, keeping the original file in case you need to refer back to your test material later. Use *this* file to enter the data for Part D.

Part D: entering/saving data and searching for information

Task 6

Open the file *without* the test data and, using the data supplied, enter the relevant details into both the Members' Table and the Trainers' Table. *Include your own name and address and choose a personal trainer.* **Accurate** data entry is essential so *proofread* each record *carefully* to check for errors.

Print one report showing all records of members, sorting them in *ascending* order of membership ID, and a second report showing the trainers' details in *descending* order of rate of pay.

Before you print **check** whether:

- The columns are wide enough to see all the data.
- The Members' Table will fit on one screen page, if necessary adjusting the margins.

Annotate the printout to explain how you designed your query.

> ***Note:*** **For each Task 7–11, produce a report from the query *indicating the task number and your own name in the header.***

Task 7

Print a list of all members' names in order of their date of birth, showing name and date of birth only.

Annotate the printout to explain how you designed your query.

Task 8

The secretary wishes to find out which members are *not* using a personal trainer so that a mail shot can be sent to them promoting the service.

Print a report giving a list of the titles, names and addresses of relevant members only.

Annotate your printout to explain how you designed your query.

Task 9

The secretary also wishes to check which members are using the tennis trainer.

Print a report showing the name of the tennis coach *only*, and the names of relevant members.

Annotate your printout to explain how you designed your query.

Task 10

Mrs Vanderwall has moved to Manchester, so delete her record from the file.

Print a report showing the names of *lady* members *only* in alphabetical order.

Annotate your printout to explain how you designed your query.

Task 11

Ms Wainwright has married Mr Albridge and their new address is 23 Merryview Court, ANYTOWN, AN6 7VC and their new telephone number is 016 6317 9001.

Print a report of these two records *only*

Annotate your printout to explain how you designed your query.

Task 12

Make a backup copy of the file.

Print screen dumps showing the file saved on the hard drive and the floppy disk.

Part E: evaluating the database

Task 13

For your actual assessment you will need to write an evaluation of your database. However, for this practice activity, discuss the evaluation with other students, either in small groups or as a whole class to compare the following points:

- Explain any problems you encountered in the design of your database and any changes you have made, or would like to make, to improve the design.
- Did you have to amend your design to include any searches?
- Which further fields or tables would improve the effectiveness of the database?
- Did you find creating a database easy/difficult, simple/complex?
- Bearing in mind you were probably inexperienced in database design, how satisfied are you with the final result?
- Any other considerations you consider important or necessary.

UNIT 2 ASSESSMENT – HANDLING INFORMATION

NOTES TO TUTORS

Two assessments have been written for Unit 2, one for database and one for spreadsheet. The specifications indicate students are required to *use* Hypertext databases, and the evidence for this should occur naturally through other activities. For example, using help files, using the Internet and the assessment for Unit 3.

We have studied the guidelines for assessment evidence and tried to write assessments which, to the best of our ability, we judge provide opportunities to generate evidence for Pass, Merit or Distinction grades.

Assessment 2.1: database

IMPORTANT NOTICE

It should be noted that if you are planning to offer the Edexcel Option Unit 10 (Database Techniques and Applications) it would be advisable to *disregard* this assessment for Unit 2. The assessment for Unit 10 includes all the material for this unit with additional material to cover the requirements for Unit 10.

If you are *not* intending to include option Unit 10, use this assessment, saved as Assess2–1.doc covering the requirements for Unit 2 (record structured databases).

Those centres not using Edexcel *may* also find the Unit 10 assessment relevant to OCR's or AQA's Option Unit 8 (Databases), although it must be stressed the additional tasks should be checked against the OCR or AQA standards. Alternatively, students designing a database for Option Unit 4 (Design Project) (offered by all three awarding bodies) may provide evidence for Unit 2 through the project.

Rationale

As you will appreciate, the concept of a relational database is quite complex. Therefore at this level we have kept the requirements as simple as possible. The database has deliberately been specified as a *record* of suppliers and products, rather than a stock control, to avoid introducing the complexities of designing an order table. You can of course include stock levels and ordering if you wish to. Guidance has been given on certain fields for the products table, which must be included, but students have a free choice of three others. This provides scope for individuality, but limits the amount of checking required.

A worked example of the database (Phones – Unit_2.mdb) is included on the CD-ROM. To illustrate the field structure, more fields have been included in the Products Table than is necessarily required by the students.

Data

Data, in the form of advertising material, is provided in Appendix 6. If you prefer you can ask the students to research all their own data, which could be a group effort. The design and implementation must still be undertaken individually. In our view it may well be easier to use the data provided, as checking database entries can be quite time-consuming, and if each student provides different source material, the time factor will be greatly increased. One task has been included for students to research a further three suppliers, including one additional phone model for each supplier. Since they need identify a small amount of new data only, this should be an individual effort rather than a group one.

Assessment

The assessment has been divided into four stages. In our experience students may be overwhelmed by a huge assessment, and also they do prefer to get on with creating a database, ignoring the planning stages. Therefore it may be advantageous to issue the four stages separately. The stages are as follows:

Part A: design.

Part B: implementation.

Part C: entering/saving data and searching for information.

Part D: evaluating the database.

Searching

Not all searches will be possible unless the student has included particular fields. This is deliberate so they amend the design if necessary to facilitate the search.

Grading criteria

A checklist has been included to identify which tasks fulfil the requirements of the three grading criteria and to provide guidelines to students on how to achieve a Merit or Distinction grade. If the design stage has been created in a simple way (e.g. text and number fields only), this may be acceptable for a Pass grade. The student may realise later that the design needs to be improved, at which point a decision can be made on whether the overall grade for this assessment can be Merit. Distinction should be reserved for students whose initial planning shows clear understanding of the complexities of database design.

It should be noted that if a student 'has demonstrated considerable effort and skill in some areas at the expense of precise detail in another' a Pass grade might be awarded, as long as 'the stated quality and sufficiency requirements have, on balance, been met'. Therefore a judgement has to be made on work which is borderline for a Pass or between Pass/Merit or Merit/Distinction grades.

Assessment 2.1: Mobile Mania – database

Tom Chattery and Iqbal Dialup want to be as efficient as possible by maximising their use of computers. They are aware that ICT Solutions has a reputation for good service and competitive rates. The manager, Iona Ternett, knows your expertise with databases and has asked you to design a database, to record the names of suppliers and the mobile phone models they plan to offer, details of which are in Appendix 6. Use copies of Form A and Form B from Appendix 2.

Part A: design

Keep a record of any problems or difficulties you encounter to assist with your evaluation. If you need to modify the design of your database at any point, make a note of this on the relevant design form, and explain why in your evaluation.

Task 1

a Use the two copies of Form A provided to plan the *design* of a suitable database file, which will provide *two related tables* – 'Suppliers' and 'Products'.

With regard to the *products* table, you *must* include the following fields:

Name of phone, phone reference, price, tariff, talktime, standby time, recharge time, weight, size, and memory.

You should then choose *three other key features* you consider important to include.

Look back to the section on 'Setting up a computerised database' in Unit 2 on page 74.

Think carefully about the following:

- The primary key for each table.
- How these two tables can be linked together.
- The other fields required.
- The length and type of field – consider carefully the best way to design the fields.
- Whether you would use a range check.
- Whether a field should be required or not.
- Which fields would be secondary keys (indexed).
- Whether either table includes a foreign key.
- Do you need a text/memo field for additional features?

b Using Form B, explain in one or two sentences why you have chosen each *different type* of field. For example, if several fields are text fields, you can give *one* explanation for choosing text for all the text fields.

c Assemble your work, which should include the following:

- A front cover entitled 'Design of Mobile Mania Database'. Insert your name and the date.
- Copies of Form A for both the suppliers and products tables.
- Form B explaining the choice of fields.

Part B: implementation

Task 2

a Make sure you have created a directory/folder for Unit 2 and a sub-directory/folder called **Assessments**. Save your work in this sub-directory/folder (see page 151 in your textbook).

b Having planned the design of your database, you should now create the two tables using the database software. Make sure you implement your design.

c Build the relationship between the two tables.

Print the relationship form.

Print the design details for both tables.

Note: If you are using Microsoft Access 97, to print the table design requested in Task 2, select the Tables tab **Tables** and from the **Tools** menu, choose:

Analyzer, Documenter Options and then select the boxes illustrated

(For Access version 2, select **File, Add-ins, Database Documenter**)

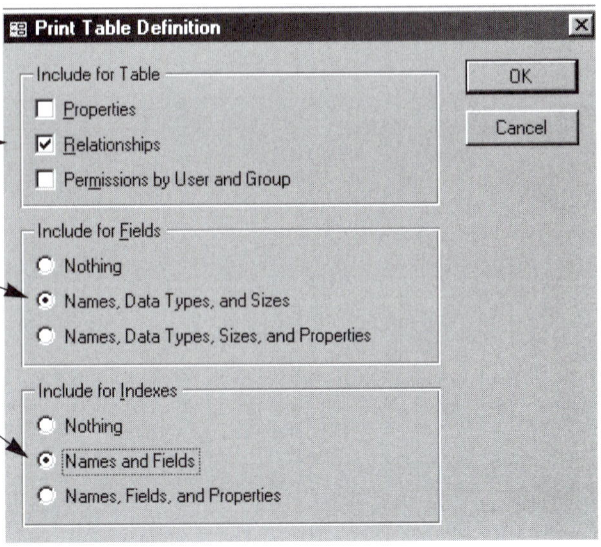

Task 3

a From the tables, create the **Form** view.

b If the software you are using is suitable, enhance the form design as you feel fit – e.g. use suitable fonts, point size, a heading, colour, shading. The form design should *not* occupy more than one screen page.

Print a copy of the form for both tables.

Save the file.

c Assemble your work, which should include the following:

- A front cover entitled 'Implementing the Design of Mobile Mania Database'. Insert your name and the date.
- Printouts of the tables (Task 2).
- Printouts of the forms (Task 3).

Part C: entering/saving data and searching for information

Note: For each of Tasks 4–10, produce a report from the query *indicating the task number and your own name in the header.*

Save all reports as Task 4, Task 5, etc.

Task 4

Enter the data into both the Suppliers' Table and the Products' Table using the data from the sheets provided in Appendix 6. Accurate data entry is essential, so *proofread* each record *carefully* to check for errors.

Print a report showing all records for *both* tables, sorting them into *alphabetical order* of suppliers, and *numerical order* of price starting with the cheapest.

Task 5

A customer is interested in phones where you buy vouchers to pay for calls. Search the database for suitable records.

Print a report listing the product reference, tariff and price in ascending order *only*.

Annotate the printout to explain how you designed your query.

Task 6

Another customer would like a phone under £80 which will allow him or her to send text messages.

Print a report in *descending* order of cost, giving the following information *only*: supplier name, contact person, telephone number, phone model, price and text messages.

Annotate the printout to explain how you designed your query.

Task 7

The model PG151 has been discontinued. Delete this record.

Print a report listing the model numbers *only* for the Speake-Easy phones.

Annotate the printout to explain how you designed your query.

Task 8

A third customer is asking about WAP phones and as he or she uses the phone a great deal, the talktime is most important and, secondly, the weight. You don't have any WAP phones in stock, but you can e-mail the supplier to find delivery dates. Search the database for suitable records.

Print a report listing the product reference, price and talktime *only* in ascending order, followed by weight in ascending order, supplier name and e-mail address.

Annotate the printout to explain how you designed your query.

Task 9

Research the Internet for three other mobile phone suppliers and choose one phone from each supplier. Enter the details of the suppliers and the phones into your database. Allocate a reference number for the three new phones. *Make sure you include your source material.*

Print *one* report listing the records for these new suppliers *only* and the details of the three phones.

Annotate the printout to explain how you designed your query.

Task 10

Design one further search of your own choice, using at least two search criteria.

Print a report of the result.

Annotate the printout to explain your search criteria.

Task 11

Make sure your database is saved in an *appropriate directory/folder* with a *suitable filename*. Make a backup copy of your file and print screen dumps showing the file saved on the hard drive and the floppy disk.

Assemble your work, which should include the following:

- A front cover entitled 'Mobile Mania Database – Data and Searches'. Insert your name and the date.
- Reports for Tasks 4–10.
- Screen dumps showing backups of your files (Task 11).

Part D: evaluating the database

Task 12

Write approximately one page of A4 (under the heading 'Mobile Mania Database – an Evaluation') evaluating your database.

Use the following subheadings:

- Introduction – see point 1 below.
- Design – see points 2 –5 below.
- Conclusion – see points 6 and 7 below.

Points to think about:

1 Briefly state the purpose of the database.

2 Explain any problems you encountered in the design of your database and any changes you have made, or would like to make, to improve the design.

3 Did you have to amend your design to include any searches?

4 Which further fields or tables would improve the effectiveness of the database?

5 Did you find creating a database easy/difficult, simple/complex?

6 Bearing in mind you were probably inexperienced in database design, how satisfied are you with the final result?

7 Any other considerations you consider important or necessary.

Assemble your work, which should include the following:

- A front cover entitled 'Mobile Mania Database – Evaluation'. Insert your name and the date.
- The evaluation of your database (Task 12).

Checklist for grading

This will help students identify the requirements to achieve a Pass, Merit or Distinction grade.

✓ Indicates the task is also required for the higher grade.

	Pass	Merit	Distinction	Checked
	The field design may be relatively simple, using all or mainly text and number fields. You may have needed quite a lot of help	The field design should be more complex. There will be no errors in data entry. Deadlines will be met, although deadlines may be renegotiated. You will have worked independently, only asking for help occasionally. Printouts will be 'well laid out, clear, easy to read and will not be unnecessarily split across pages'	The field design will show clear and in-depth understanding of the database facilities. There should be no data entry errors. The annotation of the printouts will be detailed using fluent and appropriate technical language. You will have worked independently requiring almost no help from your tutor	
Task 1	Forms A and B: • Description of user's needs • Information to be processed and processing required	✓	✓	
Task 2	• Printout of design of the tables • Relationship form	✓	✓	
Task 3		Form design – customised to improve the layout and appearance	✓	
Task 4	• Data entered correctly • Records printed	Records printed in order requested. ✓	✓	
Task 5	• Printout of search report • Printout annotated to explain query	✓	✓	
Task 6	• Printout of search report • Printout annotated to explain query	✓	✓	
Task 7	• Printout of search report • Printout annotated to explain query	✓	✓	

Task 8		Printout of search report Printout annotated to explain query	✓	
Task 9		Source information provided Data entered correctly	• Printout of search report* • Printout annotated to explain query	
Task 10			• Your own search report annotated clearly to explain its purpose	
Task 11	• Files saved correctly • Screen dumps showing backup copy made	✓	✓	
Task 12			• Evaluation of your database design, showing in-depth understanding of database systems • Clear explanation of problems encountered and improvements you made or would make	

* **To gain the Distinction grade you should produce** ***one*** report of this search rather than three reports showing each supplier separately.

Assessment 2.2: salary model

NOTES TO TUTORS

Rationale

Assessment 2.2 has been designed as a simple salary model to calculate the pay for hourly paid staff, who each week work variable hours which are recorded on timesheets. Fixed rates are given for weekday and weekend working, together with the rate for tax and insurance, which enables the students to demonstrate the use of absolute and relative cell references. A loyalty bonus is paid for staff working more than 10 hours on weekends, which provides an opportunity to demonstrate the 'If' function.

The assessment instructions are written assuming the software used will be Excel. You may find it necessary to change references to filenames if you are using another spreadsheet program.

Data

Completed timesheets for the first four weeks of trading are included in Appendix 7, *but the month and date of authorisation on the timesheets has been deliberately left blank* so you can complete the sheets with a date relevant to the month in which you issue the assessment.

Files provided

Wages.xlt – the bare bones of the template, poorly laid out, no formatting, no formulae. This is the file students should have access to as their starting point to complete the tasks.

Pay.xlt – an example of how the finished template might look.

New-Pay.xls – this is a worked example assuming the timesheets are for the month of September 2000. The date can be adjusted as already explained, depending on when the assessment is issued. Example graphs are also included.

What_if.xls – this is a worked example showing the changes if the loyalty bonus and weekly rate are increased.

Assessment

The assessment has been divided into four sections:

Part A: designing the spreadsheet.

Part B: entering the data.

Part C: creating graphs.

Part D: evaluation.

It might be advisable to issue Part A separately to check the template is a reasonable working model before students attempt to enter the data. Any help necessary at this stage can be reflected in the grading.

Grading criteria

A checklist has been included to identify which tasks fulfil the requirements of the three grading criteria and to provide guidelines to students on how to achieve a Pass, Merit or Distinction grade. When awarding the higher grades it is suggested the following key factors should be considered:

- The layout of the spreadsheet.
- The use of formatting facilities to improve the appearance.
- The ability of the student to prepare suitable formulae with little or no help.
- The annotation of the printouts, giving clear explanations of the purpose of absolute cell references, etc.

Week 1

	A	B	C	D	E	F	G	H	I	J	K	L	M	N
1	Mobile Mania Wages													
2	Month:													
3														
4	Hourly	Mon-Fri	4.30		Inc. Tax	20%		Loyalty Bc	£5					
5	Rate:	Sat/Sun	6.80		Nat. Ins.	9%								
6														
7				Hours Worked										
8	Staff Ref	First Nam	Last Nam	Mon-Fri	Sat/Sun	Weekday p	Weekend I	Sales	Commiss	Gross Pa	Tax	National Ir	Tax Refun	Net Pay
9	1	Nabil	Mughal											
10	2	Jane	Jones											
11	3	James	Corbett											
12	4	Claire	Spiller											
13			Totals											

Wages.xlt

Week 1

	A	B	C	D	E	F	G	H	I	J	K	L	M
1	Mobile Mania Wages												
2	Month:												
3													
4	Hourly	Mon-Fri	£ 4.30		Inc. Tax	20%		Loyalty Bonus:	£5				
5	Rate:	Sat/Sun	£ 6.80		Nat. Ins.	9%							
6													
7				Hours Worked									
8	Staff Ref	First Name	Last Name	Mon-Fri	Sat/Sun	Weekday Pay	Weekend Pay	Loyalty Bonus	Gross Pay	Tax	Nat. Ins	Tax Refund	Net Pay
9	1	Nabil	Mughal			0.00	0.00	0.00	0.00	0.00	0.00		0.00
10	2	Jane	Jones			0.00	0.00	0.00	0.00	0.00	0.00		0.00
11	3	James	Corbett			0.00	0.00	0.00	0.00	0.00	0.00		0.00
12	4	Claire	Spiller			0.00	0.00	0.00	0.00	0.00	0.00		0.00
13			Totals	0.00	0.00	0.00	0.00	0.00	0.00	0.00	0.00	0.00	0.00

Pay.xlt

New-Pay.xls

	A	B	C	D	E	F	G	H	I	J	K	L	M
1	Mobile Mania Wages												
2	Month:	September											
3													
4	Hourly	Mon-Fri	£ 4.30		Inc. Tax	20%	Loyalty Bonus:		£5				
5	Rate:	Sat/Sun	£ 6.80		Nat. Ins.	9%							
6													
7				Hours Worked									
8	Staff Ref	First Name	Last Name	Mon-Fri	Sat/Sun	Weekday Pay	Weekend Pay	Loyalty Bonus	Gross Pay	Tax	Nat. Ins	Tax Refund	Net Pay
9	3	James	Corbett		14.5	0.00	98.60	5.00	103.60	20.72	9.32		73.56
10	2	Jane	Jones	9	14.5	38.70	98.60	5.00	142.30	28.46	12.81		101.03
11	1	Nabil	Mughal	27.5	7.5	118.25	51.00	0.00	169.25		15.23		154.02
12	4	Claire	Spiller	12	4	51.60	27.20	0.00	78.80		7.09		71.71
13			Totals	48.50	40.50	208.55	275.40	10.00	493.95	49.18	44.46	0.00	400.31

Week 1

	A	B	C	D	E	F	G	H	I	J	K	L	M
1	Mobile Mania Wages												
2	Month:	September											
3													
4	Hourly	Mon-Fri	£ 4.30		Inc. Tax	20%	Loyalty Bonus:		£5				
5	Rate:	Sat/Sun	£ 6.80		Nat. Ins.	9%							
6													
7				Hours Worked									
8	Staff Ref	First Name	Last Name	Mon-Fri	Sat/Sun	Weekday Pay	Weekend Pay	Loyalty Bonus	Gross Pay	Tax	Nat. Ins	Tax Refund	Net Pay
9	4	Claire	Spiller	12	4	51.60	27.20	0.00	78.80	15.76	7.09		55.95
10	3	James	Corbett		14.5	0.00	98.60	5.00	103.60		9.32	12.43	106.71
11	2	Jane	Jones	9	7	38.70	47.60	0.00	86.30	17.26	7.77		61.27
12	1	Nabil	Mughal	27.5		118.25	0.00	0.00	118.25	23.65	10.64		83.96
13			Totals	48.50	25.50	208.55	173.40	5.00	386.95	56.67	34.83	12.43	307.89

Week 2

New-Pay.xls

	A	B	C	D	E	F	G	H	I	J	K	L	M
1	Mobile Mania Wages												
2	Month:	September											
3													
4	Hourly	Mon-Fri	£ 4.30		Inc. Tax	20%	Loyalty Bonus:		£5				
5	Rate:	Sat/Sun	£ 6.80		Nat. Ins.	9%							
6													
7				Hours Worked									
8	Staff Ref	First Name	Last Name	Mon-Fri	Sat/Sun	Weekday Pay	Weekend Pay	Loyalty Bonus	Gross Pay	Tax	Nat. Ins	Tax Refund	Net Pay
9	1	Nabil	Mughal	27.5		118.25	0.00	0.00	118.25	23.65	10.64		83.96
10	4	Claire	Spiller	12	11.5	51.60	78.20	5.00	134.80	26.96	12.13		95.71
11	3	James	Corbett		14.5	0.00	98.60	5.00	103.60	20.72	9.32		73.56
12	2	Jane	Jones	9	7	38.70	47.60	0.00	86.30	17.26	7.77		61.27
13			Totals	48.50	33.00	208.55	224.40	10.00	442.95	88.59	39.87	0.00	£ 314.49

Week 3

	A	B	C	D	E	F	G	H	I	J	K	L	M
1	Mobile Mania Wages												
2	Month:	September											
3													
4	Hourly	Mon-Fri	£ 4.30		Inc. Tax	20%	Loyalty Bonus:		£5				
5	Rate:	Sat/Sun	£ 6.80		Nat. Ins.	9%							
6													
7				Hours Worked									
8	Staff Ref	First Name	Last Name	Mon-Fri	Sat/Sun	Weekday Pay	Weekend Pay	Loyalty Bonus	Gross Pay	Tax	Nat. Ins	Tax Refund	Net Pay
9	1	Nabil	Mughal			0.00	0.00	0.00	0.00	0.00	0.00		0.00
10	3	James	Corbett		14.5	0.00	98.60	5.00	103.60	20.72	9.32		73.56
11	4	Claire	Spiller	12.0	11.5	51.60	78.20	5.00	134.80	26.96	12.13		95.71
12	5	Mavis	McKay	22.5	7.0	96.75	47.60	0.00	144.35	28.87	12.99		102.49
13			Totals	34.5	33.0	148.35	224.40	10.00	382.75	76.55	34.45	0.00	271.75

Week 4

Week 3

	A	B	C	D	E	F	G	H	I	J	K	L	M
1	Mobile Mania Wages												
2	Month:												
3													
4	Hourly	Mon-Fri	£ 5.30		Inc. Tax	20%		Loyalty Bonus:	£10				
5	Rate:	Sat/Sun	£ 7.80		Nat. Ins.	9%							
6													
7				Hours Worked									
8	Staff Ref	First Name	Last Name	Mon-Fri	Sat/Sun	Weekday Pay	Weekend Pay	Loyalty Bonus	Gross Pay	Tax	Nat. Ins	Tax Refund	Net Pay
9	1	Nabil	Mughal			0.00	0.00	0.00	0.00	0.00	0.00		0.00
10	3	James	Corbett		14.5	0.00	113.10	10.00	123.10	24.62	11.08		87.40
11	4	Claire	Spiller	12.0	11.5	63.60	89.70	10.00	163.30	32.66	14.70		115.94
12	5	Mavis	McKay	22.5	7.0	119.25	54.60	0.00	173.85	34.77	15.65		123.43
13			Totals	34.5	33.0	182.85	257.40	20.00	460.25	92.05	41.42	0.00	326.78

What-if.xls

Graphs

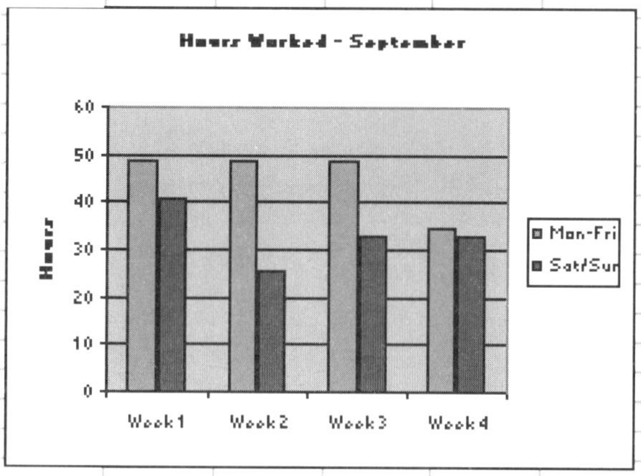
Hours Worked - September
Hours
60
50
40
30
20
10
0
Week 1
Week 2
Week 3
Week 4
Mon-Fri
Sat/Sun

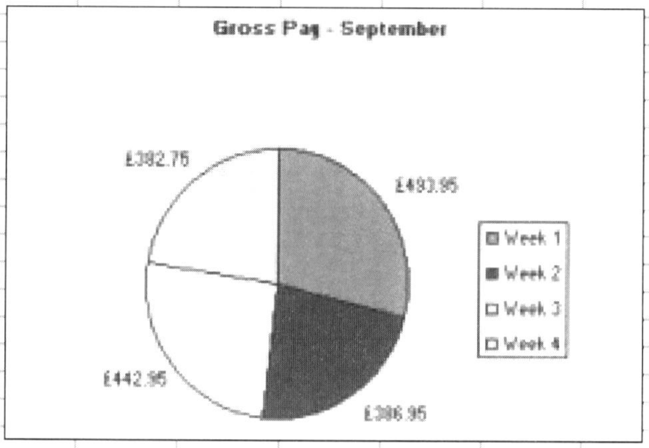
Gross Pay - September
£442.95
Week 1
Week 2
Week 3
Week 4

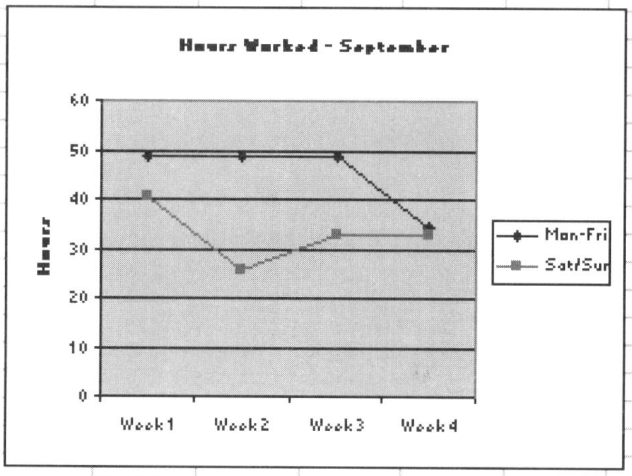
Hours Worked - September
Hours
60
50
40
30
20
10
0
Week 1
Week 2
Week 3
Week 4
Mon-Fri
Sat/Sun

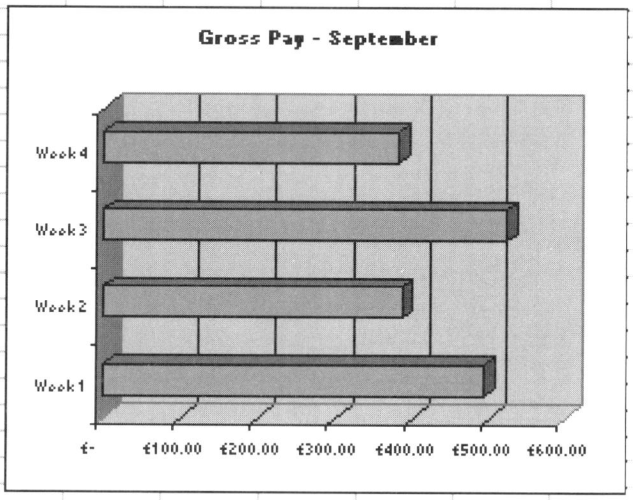
Gross Pay - September
Week 4
Week 3
Week 2
Week 1
£-
£100.00
£200.00
£300.00
£400.00
£500.00
£600.00

Assessment 2.2: Mobile Mania – salary model

Scenario

Tom Chattery and Iqbal Dialup are anxious to be as organised as possible before the shop opens. They anticipate employing four staff on an hourly basis at £4.30 per hour before deductions or any bonus. On Saturdays and Sundays the hourly rate will be increased to £6.80 per hour. They have made a start on designing a spreadsheet to keep track of staff wages, but realise they could use their time more effectively on other aspects of setting up the business. Therefore they have asked ICT Solutions to finish the spreadsheet *template* for them.

Part A: designing the spreadsheet

Task 1

a Make sure you have created a directory/folder for Unit 2 and a sub-directory/folder called **assessment** (see page 151 in your textbook) and copy the file saved as **wages.xlt** into it. *Open* it as a *template* file.

b Add your own name to the file footer (the filename and date are already entered).

Task 2

a Calculate the **Weekday and Weekend Pay** for each employee using a formula based on the hours worked and the hourly rate as an *absolute cell reference.*

b Insert formulae to calculate the **Gross Pay**.

c Insert appropriate formulae using *absolute cell references* to calculate **National Insurance** and **Tax**, which are deducted from everyone's pay by the government and are based on a percentage of the **Gross Pay**.

d Staff who work more than 10 hours on weekends are paid a **£5 Loyalty Bonus**. Insert a formula using the *If* function and *absolute cell reference* to calculate this.

e Calculate the **Net Pay** by deducting the tax and national insurance from the gross pay and adding any **Tax refunded** or **Loyalty Bonus**.

f Copy all formulae down the rows.

g Insert a formula to calculate the **Total** for **Mon-Fri Hours** and copy it across all the relevant *columns*.

h Improve the appearance of the layout using the skills you developed through Chapter 2.3 ('Spreadsheet Methods'). Use borders and shading rather than gridlines to improve the appearance. Try to keep as much of the spreadsheet as possible visible within one screen page.

i Make sure your name, the date and the filename are in the footer and the sheet name is in the header.

Save the file as a *template* file called **Pay.xlt**

j *Centre* the spreadsheet neatly on the page.

Print two copies of the *template,* one showing the *formulae* used. Close the file.

> At this stage it is vital you show your printouts to your tutor for checking as correct answers to the following tasks depend on the template being correct!

Task 3

a Once your tutor has approved your layout and formulae, *open* the file **Pay.xlt** again as a template file.

b *Copy the sheet* **Week** 1 on to sheets 2, 3 and 4 in your workbook and *rename* the sheets **Week** 2, **Week** 3 and **Week** 4. Check carefully the layout is satisfactory for the other three sheets.

Save as **Pay.xlt** and *close* the file.

Part B: entering the data

Task 4

Mobile Mania has been open for four weeks, but it has been so busy none of the staff timesheets have been entered into the spreadsheet. Open a *new* file based on the **PAY template**. Using the timesheets in Appendix 7, *enter the data* for the relevant weeks, *taking note* of the following:

Week 1

Claire Spiller and Nabil Mughal have not worked before, so do not pay any tax this week.

Sort the spreadsheet alphabetically by last name.

Save the file as a **Workbook** file called **Pay.xls**

Print a copy of the **Week 1 spreadsheet**, and another copy showing *the formulae.*

Annotate the printout to explain the formulae and how you were able to sort the data alphabetically.

Week 2

James Corbett's tax code has been wrongly assessed and therefore he has no tax to pay this week, but is due for a tax refund based on 12% of his gross pay.

Sort the spreadsheet by **Gross Pay lowest to highest**.

Save the file as **Pay.xls**

Print a copy of the **Week 2 spreadsheet** and another copy showing *the formulae.*

Annotate the printout to explain the amendments necessary and how you were able to sort the data numerically.

Week 3

Sort the spreadsheet by **Net Pay highest to lowest**.

Save the file as **Pay.xls**

Print a copy of the **Week 3 spreadsheet**.

Annotate the printout to explain the difference in sorting the data numerically from highest to lowest.

Week 4

1 Jane Jones has found a permanent job where she doesn't have to work weekends. *Delete* the *whole row* showing her name and details.

2 There is no timesheet for week 4 for Nabil as he is on holiday.

3 A new employee **Mavis McKay** has been taken on in place of Jane Jones. Add her name at the bottom of the staff list (inserting a new row if necessary). Her staff reference will be 5. Check the formulae are still correct and also any borders and shading.

Save the file as **Pay.xls**

Print a copy of the **Week 4 spreadsheet**.

Annotate the printout to explain the amendments necessary.

Task 5

The business is going so well Tom and Iqbal are considering an increase in wages. They want to see how much extra it will cost. *Amend* the spreadsheet for **Week** 4 as follows:

- Increase the loyalty bonus to £10.
- Increase the weekday rate to £5.30 per hour and the weekend rate to £7.80 per hour.

Save the file under a *new name* – **What_if.xls**

Print a copy of the **Week** 4 **worksheet**.

Annotate the printout to illustrate the benefits of using a 'What If' query.

Task 6

Make backup copies of the **Pay** template and the **Pay** and **What_if workbooks**.

Print screen dumps to show the original directory/folder and files saved on the hard drive and on the floppy disk.

Part C: creating graphs

Task 7

Iqbal and Tom would like to see comparisons in graphs or charts. Open the *original* file **New-Pay.xls** and insert a new worksheet called **Graphs**. Copy the relevant data to the graph worksheet(s).

Create a column chart and a line graph to illustrate the hours worked on weekdays and weekends for the four weeks. Include suitable axis titles and a legend.

Print the graphs and

Annotate the printouts to indicate which version you feel best illustrates the data.

Prepare a pie chart and a bar chart to illustrate the total of gross pay for the four weeks.

Print the graphs and

Annotate the printouts to indicate which version you feel best illustrates the data.

Save the file.

Part D: evaluation

Task 8

Give a short evaluation (approximately half an A4 page) of the changes you made to the original wages template, indicating why they make it easier to use the spreadsheet. Explain the advantages of using formulae rather than using a calculator and entering the results into the spreadsheet. Are there any further improvements you could make?

Assemble your work, which should include the following:

- A front cover entitled 'Mobile Mania Salary Model'. Insert your name and the date.
- Two printouts of file **Pay.xlt** – one showing the Formula view (Task 2).
- Annotated printouts for **New-Pay.xls,** Weeks 1, 2, 3 and 4 (Task 3).
- Annotated printout of **What_if.xls**, *Week 4 only* (Task 5).
- Screen dumps showing backups of your files (Task 6).
- Annotated printouts of column, pie and bar charts and the line graph (Task 7).
- The evaluation of your spreadsheet (Task 8).

Checklist for grading

This will help students identify the requirements to achieve a Pass, Merit or Distinction grade.

✓ Indicates the task is also required for the higher grade.

	Pass	Merit	Distinction	Completed	
				Student	Assessor
		Annotations show good understanding of spreadsheet systems, but not the in-depth knowledge required for a Distinction	Annotations show in-depth understanding of spreadsheet systems		
Task 1	• File copied as directed	• Headers and footers correct	✓		
Task 2	• Simple spreadsheet layout • Formulae achieved with some help	• Good effort on improving layout • Formulae achieved with little help	• Excellent use of borders and shading to improve layout • Formulae achieved with no or virtually no help		
Task 3	• Template for week 1 copied on to the other three sheets, and worksheets renamed	✓	✓		
Task 4	• Data entered correctly • Sort instructions completed successfully • Amendments correct	• Printouts annotated to explain formulae, sorting and amendments	✓		
Task 5	• Prediction correct	• Printout annotated to explain benefits of 'What If' query	✓		
Task 6	• Files saved correctly • Screen dumps showing backup copies	✓	✓		
Task 7		• Graphs created correctly with legend where suitable and titles • Printouts annotated to explain which graph best illustrates the data	✓		
Task 8			• Evaluation of the spreadsheet		

UNIT 3 ASSESSMENT – HARDWARE AND SOFTWARE

NOTES TO TUTORS

> *Note:* Activities suggested for Unit 4 (Design Project) include setting up and configuring a system for a third party. If a student has an opportunity to set up a real system, Units 3 and 4 could be combined, in which case the student would need to follow the rigorous design and planning requirements, etc., set out in Unit 4 rather than Assessments 3.1 and 3.2. He or she may need to complete Assessment 3.3 to provide the programming evidence.

Rationale

The material we are providing has been broken down into three separate sections:

- *Assessment 3.1* requires students to describe the set-up and configuration of Mobile Mania's new system.
- *Assessment 3.2* requires them to implement it (3.1 and 3.2 have been separated to allow for marking/checking Assessment 3.1 before students start 3.2).
- *Assessment 3.3* provides the opportunity for students to design and produce web pages for Mobile Mania.

From our experience with students at Intermediate level, most prefer a very structured approach and find it difficult to work too much out for themselves at one time. The assessments, therefore, ask students to extract some information for themselves (i.e. a specification for the computer system from the scenario) and give more detailed guidance for other aspects (i.e. system configuration and templates).

In order to reduce the amount of straight keying in we have tried to include some variety in the way students produce their evidence.

Grading criteria

We have produced a checklist to help students clarify the evidence requirements for Pass, Merit and Distinction, which is included with the assessment material. The checklist should also help them to ensure all parts of the assessment have been completed.

Assessment 3.1: select an ICT system

There are six separate tasks.

Task 1 requires students to read the scenario provided (Appendix 4) to determine Mobile Mania's hardware and software requirements from the descriptions contained within it. We have suggested they use the table produced for the activity in Unit 3 to record their choices. This table is available on the CD-ROM (Selecting System Table.doc) for students who did not complete the activity. A hard copy is also included as Appendix 8.

Task 2 asks students to research the Internet, computer magazines, shops, etc., to identify a computer system that meets their specification and is within budget. This information is then entered into a spreadsheet and the total cost worked out. In many cases the students will choose computers with software of limited use in a small business and we have suggested that additional software might need to be purchased which should still fall within that budget.

Task 3 gives some specific requirements in the form of handwritten notes on system configuration but also asks students to suggest other possibilities. They should consider both operating system and applications software and we have suggested the inclusion of sketches to support their written descriptions.

We would expect the directory/folder structure to resemble the following:

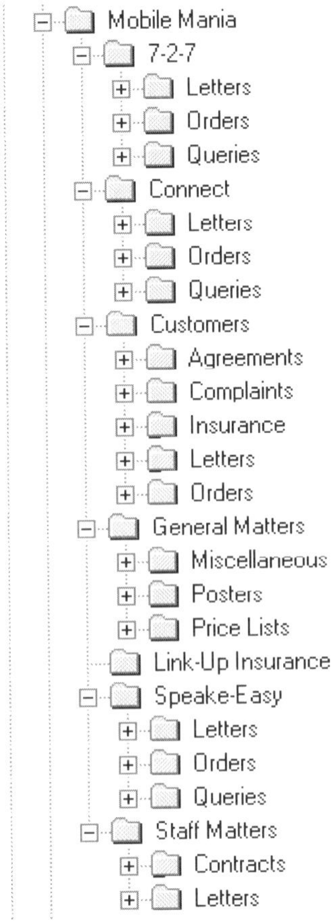

Task 4 relates to the design of templates and macros in both word processing and spreadsheet software. The assessment evidence calls for *a* suitable macro and template. However, we have suggested two macros and two templates to use both word processing and spreadsheet software. It is left to you to decide whether to amend this to suit your students. Detailed guidelines are given to help students with this part of the assessment. We have included a grid to help them plan the spreadsheet template so that formulae inserted into the appropriate cells at the design stage can be checked before implementation.

Students should provide evidence of backup copies of their files when handing in the assessment.

Assessment 3.2: set up an ICT system

Task 1 assumes most schools and colleges will have limited resources and we have suggested students use standalone equipment only to demonstrate their ability to set up a system. If necessary they can complete the remainder of Assessment 3.2 using their usual school or college computers.

A checklist is included that can be initialled to provide evidence students have demonstrated setting up the system.

Task 2 is designed to gather evidence of system configuration and can be supported with annotated screen prints to show students can configure both operating system and applications software to match their specification in Assessment 3.1. As some schools and colleges may have their systems set up to prevent students from changing settings, screen dumps identifying how the settings may be changed would provide evidence that students know how to configure software.

Task 3 calls for the creation and testing of the macros and templates designed in Assessment 3.1. We have included the production of brief user documentation as we feel this is a useful check for students to ensure their macros and templates work as designed. It can also be a beneficial exercise in preparation for other units where detailed user documentation is required.

We have suggested students provide screen dumps as evidence they have set the macros up as described in Assessment 3.1. The macros should be tested and, if necessary, annotated to show how they might be improved. Copies of the code should be included showing any amendments that have been made.

Students should set up and test the templates they designed in Assessment 3.1. Test material is included in Appendix 9. Evidence of testing should also be handed in, annotated if necessary to indicate amendments that need to be made to the template.

Finally students should evaluate their work and present evidence of backup procedures.

Assessment 3.3: write short computer programs

Students will probably enjoy this assessment more than most. We all know that, given the chance, students would happily spend all week on the Internet and, if your students are like ours, they are quite devious in hiding it! However, this assessment provides the opportunity to demonstrate their skills in designing and setting up a series of web pages for Mobile Mania using html code, text, graphic images and sound.

Task 1 – students will produce detailed sketch designs of their web pages, indicating the html tags they will use.

Task 2 – implementation of the designs and screen prints to show development, annotated to indicate changes. A copy of the html code should also be printed and this can be compared with the design in Task 1.

Task 3 – evaluation of the web pages to include comments from a third party who has used the web pages and evidence of backup.

Assessment 3.1: select an ICT system

Iona Ternett has asked you to oversee the Mobile Mania account from design through to implementation and the first thing you need to do is produce detailed and comprehensive notes describing the new ICT system.

Task 1

Read the scenario in Appendix 4, where you will find descriptions of Mobile Mania's ICT requirements. What hardware and software do they need to meet these needs?

Using the template you produced for the activity in Chapter 3.4 (when you identified the hardware and software requirements for Ian Duncan's catering business), specify *and justify* all the hardware and software components needed for their new ICT system. If you didn't create the template, a hard copy is included in Appendix 8 or your tutor has soft copy on CD-ROM.

Print a copy of the specification.

Task 2

Once you have listed all their requirements, you must choose a real system that meets your specification.

Using up-to-date computer magazines, shops, the Internet, etc., research computer systems and select one that matches the specification produced in Task 1. Make sure the system you choose falls within the £2,500 budget Mobile Mania has set. Hand in a copy of your source material with your assessment.

Look carefully at the software included with the system. Will it enable Mobile Mania to do *everything* they have described and you have specified? You might have to buy additional software to meet their requirements fully. If so, you must make sure the cost of the hardware *plus* any additional software still falls within the budget.

Using a spreadsheet, enter full details of the specification of your chosen computer system showing the cost of individual components and the total cost of the system, including any additional software. Choose suitable row and column headings and use the formatting tools to enhance the presentation.

Print the spreadsheet and hand in a second copy showing the formulae you have used.

Task 3

Before Tom and Iqbal can make full use of the new computer system it must be configured to meet their needs. Configuration is twofold:

a Configuration of the *operating system software* should include the following:

- Time and date.
- Security passwords.
- Anti-virus checks.
- Screen prompts.
- Desktop appearance.
- Mouse settings.
- Directory/folder structures.

Iona has given you a copy of handwritten notes she made when talking to Iqbal and Tom. These identify specific needs which should be taken into account when describing the operating system software configuration you propose.

Produce a written description of the work that will be required and include sketches to illustrate your proposals, if appropriate. Identify the specific areas of the computer you will access to make your changes (e.g. Explorer or File Manager to create the directory/folder structures).

Here are Iona's notes:

> *We discussed system configuration (Iqbal is left-handed) and specifically Iqbal would like security passwords to be set up and a screen saver with the words 'Welcome to Mobile Mania' in black/red to cut in after 2 minutes. We must also set up directories/folders for:*
>
> - *General matters (ie price lists, posters, miscellaneous)*
> - *Customers (including Agreements, Letters, Orders, Complaints, Insurance)*
> - *Each of the Suppliers (orders, queries and letters)*
> - *Staff matters (letters and contracts)*
> - *Dealings with Link-Up Insurance.*
>
> *I leave you to decide what other configuration should be recommended.*

b Configuration of the *applications software* will include the following:

- Setting spell and grammar checks.
- Setting/modifying default templates.
- Setting backup methods.
- Setting suitable printer drivers.
- Toolbar display and layout.
- Setting display parameters.
- Setting default file locations.
- Setting scroll bar and status bars.

Look at Iona's notes below and incorporate these specific requests into your proposals. Produce a written description of the work that will need to be done and include sketch illustrations if appropriate. Identify the menus, etc., you will use to modify the applications software settings.

> *Toolbar to be in set to centimetres*
>
> *Normal style to be Arial 11 pt*
>
> *Regular back-up required*
>
> *Automatic save every 10 minutes*
>
> *Check default locations – files should default to General*
>
> *Plus anything else you think appropriate.*

Task 4

Tom and Iqbal know very little about their application software and Iona has proposed macros and templates to help them make more effective use of it.

At this stage you do not have to produce the macros or templates but your written descriptions will clearly enable somebody else to produce them if necessary. You might need to include sketches showing how the finished products will look and must give details of the filenames/paths or macro names/icons/shortcut keys you will use when you set them up.

a *Design* a macro and template for word processing software.

Here is Iona's note about the first macro:

> *Macro to insert a mobile phone watermark as background on A4 paper. This can then be used as a temporary letterhead until they are able to have new design completed – also useful for printing price lists etc. Suggest you choose something in standard Clip Art.*

Here is the information about the first template:

Mobile Mania are going to offer customers mobile phone insurance and they have negotiated a deal with Link-Up Insurance International of City House, Moor End Lane, London WC2A 4BG. Customers must be given a copy of a declaration and Iona suggested a template could be set up which could be completed in the shop and printed straight away when customers buy their phone.

Tom has produced the following handwritten draft to show the information that should be included in the template. Iona suggested the macro could be used to insert the watermark on the declaration.

Mobile Mania Letterhead

Mobile Phone Insurance

underwritten by

Link-up Insurance International

(put in the address)

Customer Name:

Address :

Postcode :

Mobile phone No: Tariff:

Model Reference: Serial No:

DECLARATION

Have you ever, in respect of this type of insurance:

	YES	NO
Sustained any loss(es)?	☐	☐
Had any insurance declined, cancelled or refused?	☐	☐
Had any insurance subject to special terms?	☐	☐

If the answer to any question is YES, please give details

[ ]

This declaration to be read, signed and dated by the customer

I declare that the information I have given is true and complete and this application will be the basis of a contract between me and the insurer.

Signed (Customer) Dated

COVER WILL COMMENCE ON THE DATE THIS APPLICATION IS SIGNED BY MOBILE MANIA

Signed (Mobile Mania) Dated

b *Design* a macro and template for the spreadsheet software.

Iona's notes below indicate an order form would be useful and she has set out details of the layout required by Mobile Mania.

Here is Iona's note about the spreadsheet template:

It will also be useful to create an Order template which Tom and Iqbal can use each time they order new stock from suppliers. It should include built-in facilities to calculate the cost of each order and will show Mobile Mania's address, Order Number and Date with space for the Supplier's name and address. The order should have the following headings and sufficient space should be left to complete the order with several items.

Quantity Ordered	Reference Number	Description	Price Each	Total Cost
			Sub Total	
			Plus VAT @ 17.5%	
			Order Total	

Use the worksheet provided to plan your spreadsheet template. Work out where you will need formulae and write the formulae in the correct cells.

Here is the information about the spreadsheet macro:

When you have designed the order template, describe a macro you will write that will enable Iqbal and Tom to open the order automatically and insert the current date into it. Your description should enable somebody else to produce it if necessary and must give details of the macro names/icons/shortcut keys you will use when you set it up.

Task 5

Make backup copies of your data files on a floppy disk.

Print screen dumps to show the files saved both on the hard drive and backed up on disk.

Task 6

Assemble details of the new computer system for submission to your tutor. You should include the following:

- A front cover entitled 'Mobile Mania – Specification – New Computer System'. Insert your name and the date.
- Your specification for hardware and software.
- Spreadsheets showing details of your chosen computer system (include one copy showing formulae), together with your source material showing details of the recommended computer system.
- Your descriptions of the configuration you will apply to the operating system and applications software.
- Descriptions of your macro(s) and template(s).
- Evidence you have regularly saved your work using sensible filenames, in appropriate folders, and that you have produced backup copies of the files.

Spreadsheet worksheet for template design

	A	B	C	D	E	F
1						
2						
3						
4						
5						
6						
7						
8						
9						
10						
11						
12						
13						
14						
15						
16						
17						

Assessment 3.2: set up an ICT system

Tom and Iqbal have approved your proposals for the design and implementation of the new system for Mobile Mania. The hardware and software has been delivered to their shop and your next job is to install the hardware and software and set the system up in line with your proposals in Assessment 3.1.

Task 1

Demonstrate to your tutor you can safely connect the hardware components of the computer system. Power the system up, install and test software and access both the operating system and applications software. Ask your tutor to sign the attached checklist when you have demonstrated this to him or her.

Task 2

Configure the operating system and applications software to match your specification.

Print screen dumps to show how you do this.

Annotate the screen dumps to identify the settings you have specified.

Task 3

You must implement and test the macros and templates designed in both the word processing and spreadsheet software.

Macros

Print a copy of each macro.

Annotate the copy to show how you might improve them.

Print copies of the macro code before and after editing

Annotate the copy to show how you have modified or corrected the programs.

Include an annotated screen dump to show the macro buttons on the toolbars (if appropriate) and the Record Macro and Customise Keyboard dialogue boxes to confirm the names of the macros, the descriptions and the shortcut keys you have assigned to the macros.

Produce simple user documentation to enable Iqbal to locate and run the macros.

Print the documentation.

Save with suitable file names.

Templates

- Create the templates to match your designs.

  Print copies of the templates.

- In addition, provide a screen dump of your template folder to show you have saved the templates with the correct filenames.
- Test your templates by using the notes contained in this file. You will see from Appendix 9 that some customers have taken out mobile phone insurance. They need copies of the new declarations and you can prepare these to test your template.

  Print copies to hand in with the assessment.

- You will also see a note from Tom to Iqbal (Appendix 10) asking him to order some new equipment. Iqbal has noted he has placed the order by telephone and must confirm in writing. Use your new order template to do this.

  Print in a copy of the order and hand in with your assessment.

Annotate the copies to show how improvements might be made in the future.

- Produce simple user documentation to enable Iqbal to locate, use and save documents created from the templates.

Print the documentation.

Save with suitable file names.

Task 4

Before you hand the assessment in you should evaluate your work. Write between one half to a full A4 page considering the following:

- *Operating system configuration* – did you manage to complete everything you had specified? Did you manage it by yourself or did you ask for help? Have you found out anything you did not know before?
- *Applications system configuration* – again, did you manage to complete everything you had specified? Did you manage it by yourself or did you ask for help? Have you identified ways you can make your own applications software more effective for you?
- *Macros* – did they work first time? Did you need to modify the code? Did you ask your tutor or a friend to try to run them using your user documentation? Were they successful? What improvements might you make next time?
- *Templates* – were these easier to create than the macros? Were your sketch designs accurate and a help to you when creating the templates? Were the templates helpful when you produced the test declarations and order? Did you ask your tutor or a friend to try to use them following your user documentation? Were they successful? What improvements might you make next time?

Task 5

Provide evidence you have saved the test material and user documentation in addition to the templates and macros. Make backup copies of your data files on a floppy disk.

Print screen dumps to show the files saved on both the hard drive and on disk.

Task 6

Assemble your evidence of implementing and testing the new system for submission to your tutor. You should include the following:

- A front cover entitled 'Mobile Mania – Implementation and Testing – New Computer System'. Insert your name and the date.
- The page signed by your tutor confirming you have set up a computer system.
- Annotated screen dumps confirming configuration to the operating system and applications software.
- Copies of each macro, macro code and a screen dump to confirm macro names, descriptions, shortcut keys assigned and/or toolbar buttons.
- A copy of your macro user documentation.
- Copies of your template(s) and the tests you have applied.
- A copy of your template user documentation.
- The evaluation of your work.
- Evidence you have regularly saved your work using sensible filenames, in appropriate folders, and that you have produced backup copies of the files.

Assessment 3.2

Task 1

Student's name:		
Date of assessment:		
	Initials	Comments
Hardware components of the computer system have been connected safely		
The system has been powered up		
Software has been installed		
Software has been tested		
Operating system software has been used		
Applications software accessed		
Signature of Assessor:		

Assessment 3.3: write short computer programs

Mobile Mania would like to set up several web pages to advertise their new business and to introduce customers to the service they can offer.

You have been given total freedom in the design of Mobile Mania's new web site and can use the opportunity to demonstrate your newly acquired skills in web page design.

Your pages should be attractive, easy to read and easy to use and should combine text, sound (if your system has a sound card) and graphic images. The user should be able to move easily between the pages using button, graphic and/or hot spots.

Task 1

Produce detailed *sketch* designs of each of your web pages indicating the text, graphics and hot spots, etc. Include details of the html tags you will need to use.

Task 2

Produce your web pages from these designs.

Print copies of the different versions of each page to show their development.

Annotate the copies to show changes you need to make.

Print copies of the html coding for each of your finished pages.

Task 3

Write a short paragraph to evaluate the programming when you have completed it. Consider:

- Were your sketch designs detailed enough to enable you to transfer your ideas to the computer without any difficulty?
- Did you produce your pages in html code using Notepad, the Web Page Wizard or Word? Why did you choose your method?
- Which method would you choose next time? Why?
- Did the hot spots work?
- Have you asked your tutor or a friend to use your web pages? Were they able to navigate easily from one page to another?
- If you were asked to design another set of web pages, what changes would you make or what would you do the same? Explain your reasons.

Task 4

Assemble your evidence of web page design and implementation for submission to your tutor. You should include the following:

- A front cover entitled 'Mobile Mania – Web Page Design – New Computer System'. Insert your name and the date.
- Detailed *sketch* designs for each of the web pages.
- Copies of the web pages at each stage of their development.
- Copies of the html coding for each of the pages.
- An evaluation of your web pages – including comments from a third party who has used them.
- Evidence you have regularly saved your work using sensible filenames, in appropriate folders, and that you have produced backup copies of the files.

Evidence checklist

You need to produce a description of the user requirements, a hardware and software specification and an operational ICT system configured to meet user needs. The provisions for the user must include a suitable macro and template and an html program of several pages of information.

The following table illustrates the evidence requirements to determine Pass, Merit or Distinction.

To achieve a **PASS** your work must show	To achieve a **MERIT*** your work must also show	To achieve **DISTINCTION*** your work must also show	Checked ✓
Clear descriptions of the user requirements and the basic specifications for input devices, output devices, processing unit, operating system, applications software and configuration requirements, including descriptions of macros and templates	Accurate and easy-to-read descriptions of the hardware and software with detailed definitions of input and output devices You have checked the accuracy of your work and corrected obvious errors	Notes that are well written, accurate, comprehensive with fluent use of technical terms that justify your choice of system.	
The operating sytem is configured appropriately, creating directory/folder structures and setting time, date, mouse, keyboard and printer devices correctly to meet user needs Applications software is configured appropriately, setting up file locations, tool bars, backup timing, spell checker, macro and template correctly to meet user needs (printed copy or screen dumps appropriately annotated will show your skills)	You can make skilled and efficient use of the operating system, application software software and online help facilities A clear description of the macro and template, annotated to describe their purpose and how they work An attempt at producing user documentation	You have designed and configured customised toolbars and keyboard actions that are well matched to user needs and lead to significant improvements in user efficiency You have produced an imaginative and accurate template and macro that clearly enable improvements in the efficiency and effectiveness of the user and facilitate high-quality output User documentation enables the user to easily access and use the macros and templates Through annotated copies of the code before and after editing, that you have edited program code to modify or correct the program	

To achieve a **PASS** your work must show	To achieve a **MERIT*** your work must also show	To achieve **DISTINCTION*** your work must also show	Checked ✓
You can work safely when setting up equipment, check the accuracy of your work and keep backup copies of all files	Work saved in correct location using suitable file names	✓	
A basic design plan of the html program and suitable text, images, sound, control buttons and hot spots to link the pages	A clear description of several html pages containing text, images and sound with anchor tags, to link the pages and provide a means of navigation	Several attractive, easy-to-read, easy-to-use html pages of information that make good use of text, sound and graphic images and enable the user to move easily between the pages using button, graphic and textual hot spots and containing comments explaining the program	
	You can work independently to produce your work to agreed deadlines by carrying out your work plans effectively. Progress should be monitored, delays explained and deadlines renegotiated	✓	

*To achieve a Merit or Distinction, you need to improve the quality of your work but do not necessarily have to produce more work.

UNIT 4 ASSESSMENT – DESIGN PROJECT

NOTES TO TUTORS

This unit gives students the opportunity to work on an ICT project they are interested in which will also enable other ICT users to be more effective in their work or improve the quality of their output.

Initially, students should consider several ideas before deciding on one they would like to pursue and develop. We have designed a series of templates to simplify and encourage the development of ideas – these were introduced in Unit 4 and are included in this file in both photocopiable and data format.

Our intention is that the headings on the templates will help students consider all aspects relevant to the design of their project and this, in turn, should help them produce the documentation required as evidence for assessment. Approximately 25% of the time allocated to this unit is expected to be spent producing the project proposal.

Note: Ideally, students will negotiate individual or group design projects. However, opportunities for this are often limited, in which case it may be necessary to suggest topics for a design project. Our opinion is that Unit 4 could be combined with other units. For example, it could link with Unit 6 (Graphics) or Unit 12 (CAD) as a project to extend and refit Mobil Mania's shop, design a new logo and produce advertising flyers. It could stand alone to provide an opportunity for students to extend their web pages. It could be combined with Unit 3 if a student had the opportunity to help someone choose and configure a real computer system.

Rationale

We have broken the assessment down into three stages:

- *Assessment 4.1* – project proposal.
- *Assessment 4.2* – project design.
- *Assessment 4.3* – project implementation, testing and evaluation.

Students are expected to identify several ideas for possible projects. However, knowing how difficult it can be for students to come up with one idea, let alone two or more, we suggest they work either in small groups or as a class to brainstorm possible projects. We have produced a 'handout' ('Suggested topics for design projects') designed to instigate discussion within the class. It includes ideas for projects reproduced from Unit 4 in the textbook plus additional ideas – some designed to link in with other units and others to be independent.

We have designed a series of templates students can use to help them with their design project. Some can be photocopied and filled in by hand. Others can be retrieved and completed directly on to the computer to provide a variety of activities for the students.

Assessment 4.1, therefore, encourages students to consider initial ideas for their design project and to develop one idea into a full proposal.

Ideas resulting from the group discussion can be noted by hand on the 'Project identification' template. Students can then choose one of these ideas for their project and develop the theme using the 'Project proposal' template. This, together with a time plan, will form the basis of their proposal. If two copies of the time plan are produced, one can be used to monitor progress.

We have suggested that agreement to proceed be discussed at a meeting between you and each student (or group) and have included a 'Project submission' to accompany each proposal. This can be used by you for making suggestions that might improve the project and finally for recording your agreement to it.

Assessment 4.2 leads students through the design process. Again, in order to simplify the project, we have produced a template called 'Project design' that will help students plan each separate task within their project. They are also advised to produce a monitoring sheet to help them work through the project in a logical order and a test log listing the tests they will apply to their systems.

Assessment 4.3 follows the implementation, testing and evaluation of the project. Again a template is available to help design the tests, record the results and finally to evaluate the project.

The templates used can be combined with the results of tests, annotated screen prints and user documentation to form the final project documentation.

Grading criteria

We have produced a checklist to help students clarify the evidence requirements for Pass, Merit and Distinction and this is included with the assessment material. This should help them to ensure all parts of the assessment have been completed.

Suggested topics for design projects

Projects might stand alone or require a combination of several simple facilities to help someone who is unfamiliar with computers and their possibilities. A combination from the following list could make a project of a suitable size:

- Creating file and folder structures to let users store and retrieve their work easily.
- Setting toolbars in software to let users access a facility easily.
- Creating macros and templates to let users work more efficiently.
- Setting the options in software to suit users' needs.
- Creating files of commonly used text or graphics for others to use as required.
- Creating icons or files to let users access an information service quickly.
- Writing simple instructions to tell users how to use your project.
- Use of a scheduler, journal or calendar to take actions or to prompt at a given date or time.
- Creating a database or spreadsheet for a specific purpose.
- Using vector or bitmap graphics to design logos, stationery, etc.
- Using a digital camera to produce images to illustrate a brochure or promotional material.

Ideas for projects that might in themselves produce sufficient evidence are as follows:

- Producing standard design and layout templates for a magazine, including logos and page settings plus macros to insert such items as graphic images or advertisements.
- Producing a web site with multiple pages. This might be to publicise a business or leisure interest and would include hyperlinks to make the site user-friendly. It could include scanned images, digital photos or other graphics together with sound effects if the system is capable of this.
- Designing a system to keep sports club membership records. This might include the design of an application form to enable relevant data capture from new members together with a relational database to record personal details and pictures of each member, their payment details and sports activities. It would involve the design of queries and reports.
- Producing a database of work contacts, friends and relations. Setting up a facility to merge addresses in labels and letters and produce lists of telephone numbers, birthday reminders, etc.
- The production of new course leaflets for the school or college giving details of the various GNVQ Intermediate certificates offered. This would be too much for one person to complete in a limited time and so it could be shared amongst two or three students.
- Perhaps a student could work with a local business (e.g. a hairdresser) to produce price lists, appointments cards, posters, etc.
- Perhaps a local primary school might appreciate having some worksheets designed. With their pupils using computers more and more, some worksheets on a computer theme might be helpful to remind the children of what they have learnt.
- Is there a forthcoming school or college event/open evening that could offer opportunities for a design project? Producing a multi-media presentation about the school or college/GNVQ course, for example, or producing a guide to the event plus evaluation forms/posters.
- Could students work with school or college marketing to contribute to the prospectus?
- Opportunities to help family relatives or friends. For example, a guide to help someone get used to the Internet.

- Is there a local amateur dramatic society with forthcoming events? Could student(s) produce:
  - a programme
  - tickets
  - flyers
  - membership records
  - application forms?

Links with other option units could be:

- *Unit 6 (Graphics)* – plans for the extension of Mobile Mania's shop and design of a new logo, etc.
- *Unit 7 (Multimedia)* – Mobile Mania would like a presentation to introduce customers briefly to the different tariff options available and for customers then to have the opportunity to switch between the three tariffs to find out more detail.
- *Unit 9 (Modelling Numerical Information)* – an idea for one of the two projects might be the design of an invoice for Mobile Mania with look-up tables to insert prices. Could involve absolute cell reference (VAT) plus skills in formatting.
- *Unit 12 (CAD)* – a close link with the Unit 6 project for ideas.

Assessment 4.1: project proposal

When you have completed this first assessment you will have produced a design proposal for a project that interests you and you will have discussed the proposal with your tutor and obtained approval for it. The project proposal is a major part of the assessment evidence for Unit 4 and you will spend about 25% of the total time allocated to the project working on this part of it.

We have produced a series of templates that will help you plan your project and your tutor has copies of these available on disk. We suggest you refer to Unit 4 in your textbook to remind yourself of the project requirements.

It would be sensible to create a folder/directory for the design project in which to save all your work and to make backup copies of your files.

Task 1

In small groups think about ideas for possible design projects and list them on the 'Project identification' sheet.

Task 2

From the list you have made, choose one idea for a project that interests you and that you think you can complete in the time available. Before you can start work on the project you will need to think carefully about the following:

- A description of what the user wants.
- What you need to find out before you can start the project.
- How you will collect this information.
- What resources you will need.
- What tasks you will need to carry out in order to complete the project.
- What the final outcome of your project will be.

Use the template entitled 'Project proposal' to record this information.

Task 3

You must ensure you can achieve everything you need to do in the time you have available.

Use the attached 'Time plan' to list the individual tasks that will make up your project. List everything from design through to completion and estimate how long you think each task might take you to complete. Shade in the days you plan to work on each part of the project. It might be useful to make a second copy of the time plan to refer to when you set the system up to help you monitor your time.

Task 4

Word process between half and one page of A4 outlining the project and how it will benefit the user. Explain why the project interests you, and how you intend to undertake the work.

Task 5

Assemble your project proposal for submission to your tutor. It should include the following:

- A front cover entitled 'Project proposal'. Insert the title of your project together with your name and the date.
- The description of the project written for Task 4.
- The project proposal template you have completed.
- Any diagrams/sketches you have produced to support your proposal.
- The time plan listing all the tasks and showing the proposed allocation of time.
- The list showing all the projects you considered with your group.
- Screen prints to show you have saved your data files and made backup copies on disk.

When this has been completed, arrange a meeting with your tutor to discuss your proposal. Complete the 'Project submission' and hand your project proposal in to your tutor before the scheduled meeting.

PROJECT IDENTIFICATION ....

Your name: .... **Date:** ....

Your project should help someone make better use of a computer in order to be more effective in his or her work or to improve the quality of his or her work.

Who is the project for?	What is the required product?	How will it improve the user's use of ICT?	How long will it take?	What ICT design is involved?	Reasons to continue with the idea	Reasons to abandon the idea	Continue? Yes/no

PROJECT PROPOSAL

Your name: .... **Date:** ....

Project title: ....

Use this sheet to make notes to help you put your project proposal together.

A description of what the user wants		
What do I need to find out before I can start this project?		
Brief but clear description of the tasks you will carry out and the expected results		
How will I collect this information?		
Speaking to people?	*Books/manuals, etc.?*	
What resources will I need?		
People	*Books/manuals*	*Consumables*
Hardware – input devices	*Hardware – output devices*	*Software*
Description of the output or results expected (attach sketches to support your ideas)		

TIME PLAN

Your name: .... **Date:** ....

Project title: ....

Start date: .... **Finish date:** ....

List all the steps from design to completion of the project, indicating how long you anticipate each step will take. Remember to include time to test your product and to produce any user documentation.

List each task you will have to complete	Hours allocated	Duration of Project (in days)																												
		1	2	3	4	5	6	7	8	9	10	11	12	13	14	15	16	17	18	19	20	21	22	23	24	25	26	27	28	29
Total anticipated hours																														

PROJECT SUBMISSION

Name: .... **Date:** ....

Project title: ....

Date/time of meeting with tutor to discuss project proposal: ....

Points arising from discussion of project proposal

Project approved:... **Date:** ....

Assessment 4.2: project design

Now you have obtained approval for your project you must think about the design of *each* stage of the project in more detail.

Task 1

In Assessment 4.1 you produced a time plan listing everything you had to do to complete the project. Each of these tasks now has to be planned in more detail. You need to think about the following:

- What *each* particular task is designed to achieve.
- What information you will have to collect and where it will come from.
- What resources are needed for *each* task.
- The detailed design of *each* task, including sketches/illustrations.
- Where you will save your work.
- How you will check the accuracy of your work.
- How you will test your product.

Use the 'Project design' template to record this information for *each* task. You will have several pages by the time you have finished. Produce sketches and detailed illustrations where applicable (for example, designs of your web pages or the layout of the screen) and attach them to the relevant pages.

Use the 'Test log' to outline the tests you intend to carry out.

Print two copies – one to hand in with your design notes and the second to record the results of the tests when you carry them out.

Task 2

No matter how well prepared we think we are, most jobs do not go strictly according to plan. To make sure you can complete your project in the time you have available, it is advisable to prepare a checklist now that will help you monitor your time as you implement your design.

Record each task on the 'Project monitoring' template, using the same numbers you used on your design sheets.

Task 3

Assemble your project design for submission to your tutor. It should include the following:

- A front cover entitled 'Project design'. Insert the title of your project together with your name and the date.
- A sheet for each task showing your detailed design notes together with any diagrams/sketches in support of these written notes.
- A copy of the test log.
- A copy of the project monitoring sheet.
- Screen print to show you have saved your data files and made backup copies on disk.

PROJECT DESIGN

Your name: .... **Date:**...

Task No: .... **Description:** ....

Use this sheet to plan each stage of your project in detail.

What is the objective of this task – what do you want to achieve?	
What information do you need to collect? Where will you collect it from?	
Information	*Source*
What resources do you need to complete this task?	
Hardware – input devices	*Hardware – output devices*
Software	*Other*
Describe your design and attach detailed illustrations to show layout, formulae, images, records/data types, relationships, search or sort requirements, etc. (as applicable)	
Where will you save your documents? State paths/folders/filenames	
How will you check the accuracy of your work?	
How will you test your product?	

TEST LOG

Your name: .... **Date:** ....

Task No: .... **Description:** ....

Use this sheet to plan and record the tests you carry out on each part of your product.

Describe the tests you will carry out to ensure your product works

What non-computing test will you apply to your product?

Enter details of tests carried out	**Result**

What modifications were carried out?

What happened when you re-ran the tests?

How did you try to stop your design working?	**What was the result?**

PROJECT MONITORING

Your name: .... **Date:** ....

Project title: ....

List all the tasks in the order you will do them to enable you to complete your project. (Remember to include the time to produce user instructions and full project documentation.) Indicate the time you think each stage will take you to complete. Use this sheet to monitor your progress throughout your project. Tick each item when you complete it.

	Task	Start date/ hours	End-date	Changes to plan. Give reasons	Revised end-date	✓
1						
2						
3						
4						
5						
6						
7						
8						
9						
10						
11						
12						
13						
14						
15						

Assessment 4.3: project implementation, testing and evaluation

At last all the preparation is complete and you can now set up the new systems you have planned and described.

Task 1

Work through the tasks in the order you have specified on the 'Project monitoring' template.

Note any changes you make to your plan and give reasons for them. Indicate revised timings if necessary. When you have completed each task tick it off.

Print evidence to show you have completed each task (This may be in the form of screen dumps or prints).

Annotate the screen prints to explain what you have done and to indicate any changes that need to be made.

Record the results of your tests on the test log.

Print evidence wherever possible.

Annotate to show any changes that have to be made.

Produce user documentation as specified in your design and *carefully check* the accuracy of the instructions.

Task 2

Perhaps the most important part of any project is to evaluate the work you have undertaken so you understand why some parts were more successful than others. You need to consider the following:

- How well does your finished product meet its specification?
- Did you manage to achieve your work in line with your original time plan?
- What works well or less well with your product?
- How does your product benefit the user?
- How could you improve the product if you were to do it again?
- What new techniques have you learnt during the project?
- Could you use your design again?
- What does your product user think of the new system? To find this out you will need to think of questions to ask. The questions and answers should be included with your final project documentation.

You can use the 'Evaluation' template to record your answers to these questions.

Task 3

Assemble your project documentation for submission to your tutor. It should include the following:

- A front cover entitled 'Project documentation'. Insert the title of your project together with your name and date.
- Evidence that you have set the system up in line with your design.
- Screen prints of the tests you carried out together with a copy of the test log.
- Copies of user documentation.
- A copy of the 'Project monitoring' sheet recording any changes you made to the plan.
- Your project evaluation together with feedback from the product user.
- Screen prints to show you have saved your data files and made backup copies on disk.

EVALUATION

Your name: .... **Date:**...

Project title:...

Use the headings on this sheet to make notes before you compile your final project evaluation.

Does your finished product meet its specification? If not, why?
Did you meet the time schedule for the design and creation activities? If not, why?
What works well and what works less well in your product?
What advantages does your product offer the user (speed, quality, ease of use, etc.)?
What are the disadvantages of the product (time, cost, failures, poor specification, etc.)?
How could you improve the product with more time or better resources? Could you achieve the same result another way?
What new techniques have you learnt during this project?
Could you use your design on another computer or in another project?
What does your product user think? (You must design oral or written questions for the user to answer.) Include any written evaluations from the user in your project documentation.

Evidence checklist

You must produce project proposal notes, design plans for the project, a completed and operational project (or products) and an evaluation of the work undertaken.

✓ indicates you also meet the evidence requirements in the block to the left of the ✓.

The following table illustrates the evidence requirements to determine Pass, Merit or Distinction.

To achieve a **PASS** your work must show	To achieve a **MERIT*** your work must show	To achieve **DISTINCTION*** your work must show	Checked ✓
Clear description of the purpose of the project, the user requirements, the resources required and the proposed timescale	A substantial product that includes the selection, configuration and effective use of software to meet an identified need	That you have a broad understanding of ICT systems in an evaluation of your work. This will include a well written commentary on the views of users, the quality of the product, ways in which it could be improved and possible alternative methods of achieving similar results	
Clear design plans that specify the timescale, what is to be produced and accurate details of each of the component parts, such as screen layouts, storage structures and processing requirements	Accurate, attractive and easy-to-read descriptions and design plans with clearly stated objectives and detailed definitions of all component parts of the project	Imaginative design ideas in your product and demonstrate it measurably improves user efficiency and/or output quality	
A working product (or set of products) that is appropriate to user needs and operates according to the design plans	✓	✓	
Which tests you used to check the operation of your product to ensure it was complete, accurate and operational	✓	✓	
That you worked safely when setting up equipment, checked the accuracy of your work and kept backup copies of all files	✓	✓	
	That you have carefully checked your work and corrected obvious errors	✓	

To achieve a PASS your work must show	To achieve a MERIT* your work must show	To achieve DISTINCTION* your work must show	Checked ✓
	That the presentation of your work was organised so that it clearly shows how you progressed from ideas and design to completion of the project	✓	
	You worked independently to produce the product and that you monitored progress against your plan to ensure it was completed within the agreed timescale	That you have adapted your work plan appropriately to overcome any problems experienced during production	

*To achieve a Merit or Distinction, you need to improve the quality of your work but do not necessarily have to produce more work.

UNIT 6 ASSESSMENT – GRAPHICS

NOTES TO TUTORS

The evidence for this unit will come from a problem that requires explanatory text in combination with creative work. The solution will comprise a blend of text, pictures and plans and will consist of at least two vector and two bitmap-type graphics.

> *Note:* We believe this unit could be combined with Unit 4 (Design Project) and the templates designed for that unit might help students with the planning and evaluation of their graphics project.
>
> Some of the assessments designed for this unit would also lend themselves to Unit 12 (Computer Aided Design), for example the shop plan or the design of the carrier bag.

Rationale

We have produced an additional short scenario to support Unit 6 which describes plans Mobile Mania has to expand its business and to extend its premises in the Millennium Shopping Centre. This is included with the Assessment 6 file and provides the opportunity for students to undertake the following:

- *Draw up the new shop floor plans.* This can be done using vector-type software or specialist design software if it is available.
- *Design a new logo for the business*, which can be incorporated on to stationery, staff uniforms and name badges. We think this gives students the opportunity to use Clip Art, work in bitmap applications and to produce freehand images of blouses/ties for the staff. Students could also clone the logo and produce a fabric design suitable for blouses for female staff and ties for the male employees.
- *The production of an organisation chart*, showing the new organisation after expansion.
- *Design a carrier bag.* This can be designed to scale using vector-type software and images can be produced showing the basic shape before it is made up into the carrier and the finished product. Students can use colour and can incorporate the logo.
- *Produce advertising flyers.* This will provide an opportunity to scan in some images of mobile phones or to take digital photos of the students' own phones. It will also provide opportunities for combining text with graphics.

Other activities that could be considered:

- A possible group activity where students independently research shop fittings and agree the new layout for the extended shop.
- The design of a new sign to go above the shop front.
- If your students have access to a specialised package for garden design, they might design a garden for a central courtyard in the Millennium Shopping Centre or an area outside, perhaps where the buses drop shoppers off.

The checklist provided should help them to ensure all parts of the assessment have been completed.

Assessment 6.1: design the new shop

Task 1 requires students to produce a written description of the problem they are solving, describing the hardware, software and techniques they will use to solve it and indicating the timescale.

Students could use the templates produced in support of Unit 4 to help with this stage of the assessment.

Task 2 calls for freehand sketch plans of units G128 and G129 before and after alterations.

Task 3 enables students to produce scaled drawings of the sketches produced for Task 2. They can, of course, copy and flip the image of unit G128 to produce the image of unit G127 and combine these images for the new floor plan. (These techniques should be included in the written description.)

Task 4 will provide an opportunity to modify the plans produced in Task 3 to show the position of fixtures and fittings within the shop. Students may have researched shop fittings, in which case they will have sizes, but we have included some information in Appendix 13.

Task 5 gives the students the opportunity to stitch 2 images together and to apply smudging and smearing techniques.

Task 6 provides the opportunity for students to evaluate their work.

Task 7 is evidence of files/backup.

Assessment 6.2: design the new logo

We have included a selection of tasks within this assessment to provide opportunities for the more able students to use the major facilities provided by graphics software. We have therefore suggested students are left to choose for themselves two tasks from Tasks 3, 4, 5, 6 and 7.

Task 1 calls for a selection of hand-drawn logos and the detailed development of one idea after discussion with the tutor. Students will identify the software, tools and techniques to be used to create it.

Task 2 asks students to implement the design, producing annotated screen prints at each stage of the development.

Task 3 is the first optional task and requires the production of business stationery.

Task 4 requires badges to be produced for the staff.

Task 5 gives students the opportunity to produce a detailed organisation chart for the expanded business.

Task 6 is designed to give able students the opportunity to create freehand graphics and use major tools such as cloning and possibly smudging/smearing and so on to design a fabric to be used for blouses/ties and show how the finished clothes might look.

Task 7 is the final optional task and is again something more able students might like to do. It requires the design of a new paper carrier bag incorporating the logo within the design.

Task 8 calls for a brief evaluation of each of the graphics produced.

Task 9 asks students to provide evidence of file management and backup.

Task 10 – the assessment is assembled under the front cover 'Design of New Logo for Mobile Mania'.

Assessment 6.3: produce advertising flyer

This assessment provides an opportunity to combine text and graphics by designing an advertising flyer and scanning in at least one image of a mobile phone or using a digital camera to capture a suitable image.

Students produce draft designs for the 3 flyers and then work with 2 other students to compare designs and agree 3 revised designs combining ideas from everyone. Each student then creates detailed notes/sketches for one of the new designs and produces the flyer with printouts to show each stage in the flyer's development.

Students should evaluate their work to describe any difficulties they faced and how they overcame them, etc.

Assessment 6: Scenario

You will remember that when Tom and Iqbal first opened Mobile Mania they had a very limited budget and could not afford to make any improvements to the shop.

In the few months their business has been open its success has exceeded their greatest expectations and they now have plans to expand the business and employ additional staff. Unit G127 in the Millennium Shopping Centre has unexpectedly become vacant and Tom and Iqbal have decided to take on a second shop unit and convert the two units into one large shop. This will require detailed plans to be drawn up to show the dimensions of the new shop and the placement of shop fittings within the new shop. (Photographs of the two shops are available in Appendix 12, which can be stitched together to show a view of the new shop.)

This expansion also provides the perfect opportunity to introduce a corporate image. Consequently, they would like a new logo designed for Mobile Mania. The effect of this will be to introduce the following:

- New business stationery.
- A uniform dress with blouses/ties for their staff made from a fabric designed around the new logo.
- Individual name badges for staff, incorporating the new logo.
- New designer-style 'strong' paper carrier bags with rope handles.

Finally, with the opening of the new premises they are planning promotional events to attract customers and will need some flyers designed to inform customers about special offers and discounts.

Assessment 6.1: design the new shop

Unit G127 in the Millennium Shopping Centre is exactly the same size as the current premises occupied by Mobile Mania but is a mirror image. This means the stock room is on the right-hand side at the back of the shop. Tom and Iqbal have plans to remove the adjoining wall to make one large shop. They will close up the existing entrance doors and make a wider entrance in the middle of the new shop. The existing stock room, kitchen and WC will be made into one large stock room and they plan to convert the stock room in the new shop into an office, retaining the kitchen and WC.

Task 1

Read the assessment through carefully to see what you have been asked to do.

Produce a description of the work needed in order to complete this assessment. Your description should include details of the following:

- The designs you must produce.
- The hardware you will use.
- The graphics software you will use to implement your designs.
- The specific tools/techniques within the graphics software and the purposes for which you will use them (e.g. draw, fill).
- An indication of your timescale for completing the assessment.
- The filenames you will give to each stage of your production and the folders in which you will save your work.

Task 2

Produce a freehand sketch to show the layout of units G127 and G128 *before* any alterations are carried out.

Produce a second freehand sketch to show the proposed layout of the new shop *after* Units G127 and G128 have been combined. Show the dimensions of the new unit.

Task 3

Using the software, tools and techniques you specified in your description for Task 1, produce scaled plans reflecting the two freehand sketches you have drawn of the shops *before* and *after* alterations.

Print copies of the plans.

Annotate them to indicate where the tools/techniques were used.

Label the plan of the new shop to show the positions of:

- the new shop entrance
- the new stock room
- the office
- the kitchen
- the WC.

Print a copy of the new plan, fully labelled.

Task 4

Make a copy of the plan and edit it to remove the labels.

Appendix 13 provides a selection of shop fittings Tom and Iqbal would like to use in the new shop. They would like to include the following:

- Counter.
- Display shelves – both on the outside walls and free-standing on the shop floor.
- A desk within the shop where the sales assistant can sit with customers to complete any necessary paperwork (e.g. printing insurance details).
- Desk and filing cabinet in the office.

Research your own shop fittings or choose fittings from the selection provided and show the positions of the fixtures, fittings and furniture in the shop and office.

Print a copy of the new plan, fully labelled.

Task 5

Your tutor has images of Units G127 and G128 in the Millennium Shopping Centre. Demonstrate your skills in image stitching to show how the new premises might look after the alterations have been completed.

Save your work.

Print.

Task 6

Produce a short evaluation of your work. You should consider the following questions:

- Did this assessment require more work than you had anticipated when you wrote your description for Task 1? If so, what did you forget to consider when you originally planned the assessment? Why do you think you forgot it?
- Were your sketch designs clear enough for you to work from?
- Were you able to reproduce them to scale?
- Did your chosen software offer you *all* the facilities you needed to complete this work?
- Would a different software application have been better? Why?
- How accurate was your timescale?

Save.

Print.

Task 7

Annotate screen dumps to provide evidence that you have saved your work with the filenames indicated in Task 1 and that you have produced backup copies of your files.

Task 8

Assemble your new shop plans for submission to your tutor. You should include the following:

- A front cover entitled 'Design of New Shop for Mobile Mania'. Insert your name and the date.
- A written description of the work you proposed to undertake in order to complete this assessment.
- Two freehand sketches to show the layout of units G128 and G129 *before* and *after* the units are combined.
- Scaled drawings produced on the computer reflecting the two freehand sketches:
  - one set annotated to show the tools/techniques used

  - one copy of the new shop showing the position of stockroom, kitchen, etc.
  - one copy of the new shop showing fixtures, fittings and furniture in position.
- Evidence you have evaluated your work.
- Evidence you have regularly saved your work using sensible filenames in appropriate folders and that you have produced backup copies of the files.

Assessment 6.2: design the new logo

Now that plans for extending the shop are under way, Tom and Iqbal have decided to establish a corporate identity.

You have been called in to advise them on this but they have given you complete freedom in the new designs.

Task 1

Produce two different sketch designs, by hand, to show your ideas for a new logo.

Together with your tutor choose one design you will develop in more detail.

Produce a detailed freehand drawing of the chosen design on a separate sheet of paper.

Annotate this drawing to show the following:

- The graphics software you will use to produce the logo.
- The tools/techniques you will use to produce each part of its design.
- The style of any lines.
- The style and size of any fonts.
- The colours/patterns you will apply.
- The filenames you will assign to each stage of its development.

Task 2

Create your design using the graphics software you have chosen. (You can include Clip Art in the design if you wish.)

Print copies to record *each stage* in its development. (Remember to save each stage with the different filenames you specified in Task 1.)

Annotate the copies to indicate any changes you decide to make to the design and say why you are changing it.

You must now choose to complete ***any two*** *tasks from Tasks 3, 4, 5, 6 and 7 below.*

Task 3

Now the new logo is designed, Tom and Iqbal would like it to be incorporated into their business stationery.

The stationery should include:

- a business letterhead
- a compliments slip
- business cards for both Tom and Iqbal.

Produce draft sketches of the new business stationery for Mobile Mania incorporating the new logo.

Produce the stationery using the graphics package, together with your word processing software.

Print copies of all the stationery (preferably in colour).

Task 4

Tom and Iqbal are keen for each member of staff to have their own name badge. They have bought a self-assembly kit to make the badges and need the badges to be designed to fit the kit. The badges will be circular and the logo and name must fit within a diameter of 6.5 cm (or $2\frac{1}{2}$ inches).

Draw the badge to size by hand and indicate where you will place the logo and staff name.

✍ Annotate your sketch to identify the tools you will use to create the badge.

Produce a template for the badge that can be used each time a new member of staff is employed.

🖨 Print two copies

✍ Annotate one copy indicate the specific tools/techniques you used to create it.

On *one* page, produce *named* badges for *each* of the existing members of staff.

🖨 Print two copies of the page.

✍ Annotate one copy to show the tools/techniques you used.

Task 5

Tom and Iqbal have decided to appoint Michael Granger as Finance Manager (reporting directly to Tom), Shubiah Begum as Shop Manageress (reporting to Iqbal), plus two more full-time sales assistants – Eleanor Holmes and Megan Gannon.

Tom will therefore be General Manager in charge of the whole business and Iqbal is the Commercial Manager. Shubiah will be responsible for all the sales assistants.

Draw the organisation chart by hand.

From this information, produce the organisation chart for the business. Include the logo within the design of the page.

🖨 Print a copy of the organisation chart.

Task 6

To help establish the corporate image, Iqbal has decided all staff will wear a new uniform. It will comprise either black trousers or skirt and the women will wear a blouse and the men a white shirt and tie made from a fabric designed around the new logo.

Design a repeating pattern, incorporating the new logo, which will be a suitable fabric for a blouse and tie.

Transfer your design to the computer.

🖨 Print two copies of your fabric designs.

✍ Annotate one copy to indicate the tools/techniques you used .

Task 7

Tom has noticed increasingly that local shops are replacing their plastic carrier bags with new designer-style paper carrier bags with string/rope handles and he would like Mobile Mania to have these showing the new logo.

The carrier bag must first be designed 'flat' so the shape can be cut from paper. Produce a cut-out flat shape of the bag and fold the paper to show how it will be assembled.

Then produce a scaled drawing on the computer to:

- Show the shape of each bag when laid flat and indicate the dimensions.
- Indicate the fold lines with broken lines on the drawing.
- Shade in the overlaps (for sticking together).
- Indicate the position of the holes for the string.

Print two copies.

Annotate one copy to show the features listed above.

Produce a 2D graphic to show how the carrier bag will look when it is assembled and incorporate the logo on the bag.

Print two copies.

Annotate one copy to show the tools/techniques you used.

You ***must*** *complete the last two tasks.*

Task 8

Write a short evaluation of each of the graphics you have produced for this assessment. You should consider the following points:

- How difficult did you find it to reproduce your hand-drawn designs on the computer?
- Did you find some software easier to use than others?
- Did you have any problems drawing to scale?
- What new techniques did you learn?
- What did you particularly enjoy/not enjoy about this assessment?

Save your work.

Print.

Task 9

Annotate screen dumps to show you have used suitable folders/directories and saved all your work at different stages of production and that you have also made backup copies.

Task 10

Assemble your designs incorporating the new logo for submission to your tutor. You should include the following:

- A front cover entitled 'Design of New Logo for Mobile Mania'. Insert your name and the date.
- Copies of the original two freehand designs.
- Detailed freehand, annotated drawings of the chosen design.
- Screen prints of your design to show its development.
- Design drawings and screen prints of the *two* tasks selected from 3, 4, 5, 6 and 7 that you have created.
- Evidence you have evaluated your work.
- Evidence you have regularly saved your work using sensible filenames, in appropriate folders, and that you have produced backup copies of the files.

Assessment 6.3: produce advertising flyers

To celebrate the opening of the extended shop, Mobile Mania are going to have a promotion week offering special deals for customers and they are particularly keen to bring in contracts from local business for multi-users.

To advertise this they want flyers to be distributed to the homes of local residents and businesses.

The promotions will be:

Free hands-free kit with all voucher phones
or
Free insurance for one year with all new 'pay in advance' phones
or
Free initial connection charges to each of the three business user tariffs.

They would like a scanned image of at least one mobile phone to be incorporated into each flyer or a suitable image captured on digital camera.

Task 1

Produce draft designs by hand for a suitable flyer to advertise *each* of the three promotions.

Get together with two other students to compare your three designs with theirs. Agree on 3 revised designs that combine ideas from each member of the group and each of you produce one of the revised flyers.

Produce a written description of the work needed in order to complete *your* part of the assessment. Your description should include details of the following:

- The hardware you will use.
- The graphics software you will use to implement your designs.
- The source of any images you will incorporate into your design.
- The specific tools/techniques within the graphics software and the purposes for which you will use them (e.g. font size/style, colour, lines).
- An indication of your timescale for completing the assessment.
- The filenames you will give to each stage of your production and the folders in which you will save your work.

Save.

Print.

Task 2

Produce the flyer using the tools indicated in your written description.

Save your flyer at each stage of production.

Print your flyer at each stage of production.

Annotate to show the tools and techniques you have used, indicating any changes you are making to the original design.

Make sure each member of your group has a copy of your finished flyer and, likewise, make sure you have copies of theirs.

Task 3

Write a short evaluation on this assessment. Consider the following:

- Did your group agree on the final designs for each of the flyers amicably? If not, what difficulties did you encounter and how did you compromise?
- If you were doing this assessment again, would you use the same tools/techniques or would you try other methods? Why?
- Did you find anything particularly difficult? If so, how did you overcome the problems?

Task 4

Print screen dumps to provide evidence you have saved your files in a suitable folder/directory and that you have made backup copies of your data files.

Task 5

Assemble your work leading to the production of the flyer for submission to your tutor. You should include the following:

- A front cover entitled 'Advertising Flyer for Mobile Mania'. Insert your name and the date.
- Handwritten drafts of *your* three proposed flyers.
- Handwritten draft of the amended flyer *you* produced.
- Written descriptions of the work you needed to do to complete the assessment.
- Screen-printed copies of your flyer at each stage of production.
- Screen-printed copies of the other two finished flyers (make sure you each have your names on them).
- Evidence you have evaluated your work.
- Evidence you have regularly saved your work using sensible filenames, in appropriate folders, and that you have produced backup copies of the files.

Evidence checklist

You will produce a portfolio showing your skills and understanding of solving graphic problems. It should include the following:

- Records of your designing, producing and evaluating graphic solutions to one or more problems, real or simulated, which are sufficiently complex to require a solution by a combination of plans, words and pictures.
- A minimum of two vector-type graphic images and two bitmap-type graphic images.

✓ indicates you also meet the evidence requirements in the block to the left of the ✓.

The following table illustrates the evidence requirements to determine Pass, Merit or Distinction .

To achieve a **PASS** your work must show	To achieve a **MERIT*** your work must show	To achieve **DISTINCTION*** your work must show	Checked ✓
Clear description of the problem you are solving, and the techniques, hardware and software you will use to solve the problems	✓	Use of fluent technical language and clear and coherent design notes, annotations and evaluation	
Use of graphic software to create images which produce an approved solution to your problems	Accuracy in the construction and organisation of elements, especially where lines and shapes join and touch	A good understanding; you can make effective use of all the major facilities provided by the various graphics software	
That you • draw, edit and fill basic shapes • import images from Clip Art libraries • incorporate scanned or digitised photographic images	Graphics which contain a variety of shapes, images drawn freehand (i.e. using a mouse, graphics tablet, etc.), colour, fills, scanned material and text to create realistic images	A variety of graphics demonstrating skilled use in a wide range of techniques e.g. cloning, smudging and smearing	
	Effective combination of the different types of graphics with textual information to form a coherent and acceptable whole	✓	
Annotated printed copy to show how you have met the above requirements	✓	✓	
In design notes, a clear progression towards your solution with copies of pictures at different stages of development	✓	✓	
That you regularly save your work and create backup copies	✓	✓	

To achieve a **PASS** your work must show	To achieve a **MERIT*** your work must show	To achieve **DISTINCTION*** your work must show	Checked ✓
	That you can work independently to produce your work to agreed deadlines by carrying out your work plans effectively	✓	
		An evaluation of your work describing what you have done, what problems you had and, explaining with reasons, any improvements you would make to the finished images	

*To achieve a Merit or Distinction, you need to improve the quality of your work but do not necessarily have to produce more work.

UNITS 2 & 10 (COMBINED) ASSESSMENT – HANDLING INFORMATION & DATABASE TECHNIQUES AND APPLICATIONS

NOTES TO TUTORS

IMPORTANT NOTICE

Edexcel Option Unit 10 (Database Techniques and Applications) builds on the requirements for Unit 2 (Handling Information – Database Methods). In our view, as the requirements for these sections of the qualification are so interlinked, it would be simpler to deliver them jointly. *Therefore, Assessment 10.1 has been planned to provide evidence for both.* Additional or more detailed tasks have been included to reflect the requirements of Unit 10, which are indicated with an * in the checklist for grading.

Those centres not using Edexcel *may* also find the Unit 10 assessment relevant to OCR's or AQA's Option Unit 8 (Databases), although it must be stressed the additional tasks should be checked against the OCR or AQA standards. Alternatively, students designing a database for Option Unit 4 (Design Project) (offered by all three awarding bodies) may provide evidence for Unit 2 through the project.

Rationale

As you will appreciate, the concept of a relational database is quite complex, especially normalisation routines. Therefore at this level we have kept the requirements as simple as possible. In our view, the diagram required for Task 1(a), should be sufficient evidence for normalisation. Students can use the examples in the textbook for guidance, but relate them to this scenario. The relationship form for Task 2(a) should be sufficient evidence for entity relationship diagrams.

To avoid introducing the complexities of designing an order table the database has deliberately been specified as a *record* of suppliers and products, rather than a stock control. You can of course include stock levels and ordering if you wish to. Guidance has been given on certain fields for the products table, which must be included, but students have a free choice of three others. This provides scope for individuality, but limits the amount of checking required.

To meet the requirements of Unit 10 for a third related table, records of customers purchasing mobile phones and an insurance policy for their phone have been added. For the purpose of this assessment we will assume customers purchase *only one phone*.

An example of the completed database (Phones – Unit_10.mdb is included on the CD-ROM. For the purpose of illustration, more fields have been included in the products table than is necessarily required by the students.

Data

Data, in the form of advertising material, is provided in Appendix 6. If you prefer, you can ask the students to research all their own data, which could be a group effort. The design and implementation must still be undertaken individually. In our view it may well be easier to use the data provided, as checking database entries can be quite time-consuming and, if each student provides different source material, the time factor will be greatly increased. One task has been included for students to research a further three suppliers, including one additional phone model for each supplier. Since they need identify a small amount of new data only, this should be an individual effort rather than a group one. Data on customer details is provided in Appendix 9.

Assessment

The assessment has been divided into five stages. In our experience students may be overwhelmed by a huge assessment, and also they do prefer to get on with creating a database, ignoring the planning stages. Therefore it may be advantageous to issue the five stages separately. The stages are as follows:

- *Part A: design.*
- *Part B: implementation.*
- *Part C: testing. (After deleting the test data, students will find the autocounter will not start at number 1. One way to overcome the problem is to delete the primary key for members and then reinstate it. Alternatively, they can allow the autocounter to continue.)*
- *Part D: entering/saving data and searching for information.*
- *Part E: user guide and evaluation of the database.*

Searching

Not all searches will be possible unless the student has included specific fields. This is deliberate so that they amend the design if necessary to facilitate the search.

Grading criteria

A checklist has been included to identify which tasks fulfil the requirements of the three grading criteria and to provide guidelines to students on how to achieve a Merit or Distinction. If the design stage has been created in a simple way (e.g. text and number fields only) this may be acceptable for a Pass grade. The student may realise later that the design needs to be improved, at which point a decision can be made on whether the overall grade for this assessment can be Merit. Distinction should be reserved for students who are able to achieve the complex searches unaided and whose initial planning shows clear understanding of the complexities of database design.

It should be noted that if a student 'has demonstrated considerable effort and skill in some areas at the expense of precise detail in another' a Pass grade might be awarded, as long as 'the stated quality and sufficiency requirements have, on balance, been met'. Therefore a judgement has to be made on work which is borderline for a pass between Pass/Merit or Merit/Distinction grades.

Assessment 10.1: database

Tom and Iqbal want to be as efficient as possible by maximising their use of computers. They are aware that ICT Solutions has a reputation for good service and competitive rates. The manager, Iona Ternett, knows your expertise with databases and has asked you to design a database to record the names of suppliers and the mobile phone models they plan to offer, details of which are in Appendix 6. They also need to keep records of customers who purchase phones with monthly tariff charges (details of relevant customers are in Appendix 9).

Part A: design

Keep a record of any problems or difficulties you encounter to assist with your evaluation. If you need to modify the design of your database at any point, make a note of this on the relevant design form, and explain why in your evaluation.

Task 1

a Following the guidelines on pages 223–224 in Unit 10, produce suitable entity relationship diagrams for the three tables 'Suppliers', 'Products' and 'Customers'. For the purpose of this assessment, assume one customer buys one phone only.

b Use the three copies of Form A provided to plan the *design* of a suitable database file, which will provide three *related tables* – **Suppliers**, **Products** and **Customers**.

With regard to the products table, you *must* include the following fields:

Name of phone, phone reference, price, tariff, talktime, standby time, recharge time, weight, size, and memory.

You should then choose *three other key features* you consider important to include.

Look back to the section on 'Setting up a computerised database' in Unit 2 on page 74.

Think carefully about the following:

- The primary key for each table.
- How these two tables can be linked together.
- The other fields required.
- The length and type of field – consider carefully the best way to design the fields.
- Whether you would use a range check.
- Whether a field should be required or not.
- Which fields would be secondary keys (indexed).
- Whether either table includes a foreign key.
- Do you need a text/memo field for additional features?

c Using Form B, explain briefly why you have chosen each *different type* of field. For example, if several fields are text fields, you can give *one* explanation for choosing text for all the text fields.

Assemble your work, which should include the following:

- A front cover entitled 'Design of Mobile Mania Database'. Insert your name and the date.
- Copies of Form A for the suppliers, products and customers tables.
- Form B, explaining the choice of fields.

Part B: implementation

Task 2

a Make sure you have created a directory/folder for Unit 10 and a sub-directory/folder called **Assessment**. Save your work in this sub-directory/folder using a suitable file name (see page 151 of your textbook).

b Having planned the design of your database, you are now ready to create the three tables using the database software.

c Build the relationship between the three tables.

Print the relationship form.

Print the design details for both tables.

Note: If you are using Microsoft Access 97, to *print* the table design requested in Task 2, select the Tables tab Tables and from the **Tools** menu, choose:

Analyzer, Documenter Options and then select the boxes illustrated

(For Access version 2, select **File, Add-ins, Database Documenter)**

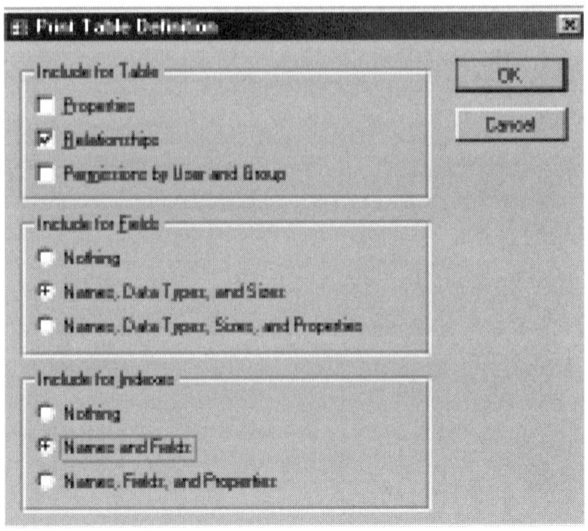

Task 3

a From the tables create the **Form** view.

b If the software you are using is suitable, add an image and enhance the form design as you feel fit (e.g. use suitable fonts, point size, a heading, colour, shading). The form design should *not* occupy more than one screen page.

Task 4

a To make your database more user-friendly to the non-technical person, design:

- An opening screen with buttons to access the different sections of the database.
- Buttons to toggle between the forms and the opening screen.
- A button to exit the database.

Print a copy of the form for the three tables and also the opening form.

Annotate the printouts to explain the benefits to users.

b Demonstrate the buttons to your tutor and obtain his/her signature on the checklist.

Assemble your work, which should include the following:

- A front cover entitled 'Implementing the Design of Mobile Mania Database'. Insert your name and the date.
- Printouts of the tables (Task 2).
- Printouts of the forms (Tasks 3 and 4).

Part C: testing

Task 5

Refer to the section on 'Testing' in Unit 10 on page 223.

a Design a log of testing for all three tables.

> You *must* use your own data for this purpose, *not the data provided.*

Don't forget to test for data which you expect to be rejected (e.g. text in a number field).

b Enter the test data from your test log into the database.

Print relevant reports from the testing.

Annotate the printouts noting any problems you encounter. If necessary, correct the design of the tables, explaining why you have made the changes.

c Once you are satisfied with your testing make a backup copy of your file.

Print screen dumps showing the file saved on the hard drive and the floppy disk.

Make a third copy of the database, giving it a *new name.* Delete all test records from this new file, *keeping the original file* in case you need to refer back to your test material later. *Use this new file* to enter the data for Part D.

Assemble your work, which should include the following:

- A front cover entitled 'Testing Mobile Mania Database'. Insert your name and the date.
- Log of testing (Task 5(a)).
- Printout of the test records (Task 5(b)).

Part D: entering/saving data and searching for information

Note: **For each of Tasks 6–13, produce a report from the query *indicating the task number and your own name in the header.***

Save all reports.

Task 6

a Enter the data into both the Suppliers Table and the Products Table using the data from the sheets provided in Appendix 6. Accurate data entry is essential so *proofread* each record *carefully* to check for errors.

Print a report showing all records for *both* tables, sorting them into *alphabetical order* of suppliers, and *numerical order* of price starting with the cheapest.

b Enter the data into the customer table using the data from the completed insurance application forms provided in Appendix 9.

Print a report showing all records in alphabetical order of the customer's last name.

Task 7

A customer is interested in phones where you buy vouchers to pay for calls. Search the database for all suitable records.

Print a report listing the product reference, tariff and price *only* in ascending order.

Annotate the printout to explain how you designed your query.

Task 8

Another customer would like a phone under £80 which will allow him or her to send text messages.

Print a report in *descending* order of cost, giving *only* the following information:

Supplier name, contact person, telephone number, phone model, price and text messages.

Annotate the printout to explain how you designed your query.

Task 9

The model PG151 has been discontinued. Delete this record.

Print a report listing the model numbers for the Speake-Easy phones *only*.

Annotate the printout to explain how you designed your query.

Task 10

A third customer is asking about WAP phones and as he or she uses the phone a great deal, the talktime is most important and, secondly, the weight. You don't have any WAP phones in stock, but you can e-mail the supplier to find delivery dates. Search the database for suitable records.

Print a report listing the product reference, price and talktime *only* in ascending order, followed by weight in ascending order, supplier name and e-mail address.

Annotate the printout to explain how you designed your query.

Task 11

Mr Patel's daughter has lost the mobile phone he bought for her. This wouldn't be covered by the guarantee, but he thinks he paid for insurance cover. Search the database to identify the model and check if he does have insurance.

Print a report listing the customer name, the mobile phone number, the serial number, the tariff and check if insurance was taken out.

Annotate the printout to explain how you designed the query.

Task 12

Using at least *two different sources* for your information, research three other mobile phone suppliers and choose one phone from each supplier. Enter the details of the suppliers and the phones into your database. Allocate a reference number for the three new phones. *Make sure you include your source material.*

Print one report listing the records for these new suppliers and the details of the three phones *only.*

Annotate the printout to explain how you designed your query.

Task 13

Design one further search of your own choice using at least two search criteria.

Print a report of the result.

Annotate the printout to explain your search criteria.

Task 14

Make sure your database is saved in an *appropriate directory/folder* with a *suitable filename.* Make a backup copy of your file.

Print screen dumps showing the original file saved on the hard drive and the floppy disk and the new file *after* testing.

Assemble your work, which should include the following:

- A front cover entitled 'Mobile Mania Database – Data and Searches'. Insert your name and the date.
- Reports for Tasks 6–13.
- Screen dumps showing backups of your files (Task 14).

Part E: user guide and evaluation of the database

Task 15

You need to write simple user documentation to explain how to use the database. *Don't give an explanation about how to design a database.* The user guide is meant to help a member of Mobile Mania staff be able to open the files, enter or delete data, etc. Therefore, your guide must explain how to:

- Access the database – what is the filename? Where is it saved?
- Move around the database interface – how to find a table, a form, etc.
- Add a record.
- Delete a record.
- Correct any errors in data entry after proofreading.
- Search for information – design a query and a report and produce the result on screen or paper.

Think about the kind of instructions you prefer. Do you like to read long sentences or do you find it easier to follow a list with numbered or bulleted points, like the list above? Screen dumps may help to illustrate important parts of the instructions.

Before you hand in your guide, test it out by following *only* the instructions you have written. You will then find out if you made any mistakes, or missed some stages.

Task 16

Write a report of approximately two A4 pages under the heading 'Mobile Mania Database – an Evaluation' to evaluate your database. Use the following subheadings:

- Introduction (see point 1 below).
- Design (see points 2–5 below).
- Security and privacy (see points 6–9 below).
- Reliability (see points 10 and 11 below).
- Conclusion (see points 12 and 13 below).

Points to think about:

1. Briefly state the purpose of the database.
2. Explain any problems you encountered in the design of your database and any changes you have made, or would like to make, to improve the design.
3. Did you have to amend your design to undertake any searches?
4. Which further fields or tables would improve the effectiveness of the database?
5. Did you find creating a database easy/difficult, simple/complex?
6. Would Mobile Mania need to register with the Data Protection Registrar? If so, explain why.
7. How can privacy of information, both personal and business, be maintained?
8. How can the security of both the hardware and software be maintained?
9. Are there any issues concerning copyright to be considered?
10. Think back to your testing.
11. How can you be sure the data is reliable – i.e. up to date?

12 Bearing in mind you were probably inexperienced in database design, how satisfied are you with the final result?

13 Any other considerations you consider important or necessary.

Assemble your work, which should include the following:

- A front cover entitled 'Mobile Mania Database – User Guide and Evaluation'. Insert your name and the date.
- The user guide (Task 15).
- The evaluation of your database (Task 16).

Checklist for grading

This will help students identify the requirements to achieve a Pass, Merit or Distinction grade.

✓ indicates the task is also required for the higher grade.

* indicates additional or more detailed tasks required for the Unit 10 assessment.

	Pass	**Merit**	**Distinction**	**Checked ✓**
	The field design may be relatively simple, using all or mainly text and number fields. You may have required quite a lot of help	The field design should be more complex. There will be no errors in data entry. Deadlines will be met, although deadlines may be renegotiated. You will have worked independently, only asking for help occasionally. Printouts will be 'well laid out, clear, easy to read and will not be unnecessarily split across pages'	The field design will show clear and in-depth understanding of the database facilities. There should be no data entry errors. The annotation of the printouts will be detailed using fluent and appropriate technical language. You will have worked independently requiring almost no help from your tutor	
*Task 1(a)	Entity relationship diagram	✓	✓	
Tasks 1(b) and 1(c)	Forms A and B: • Description of user's needs • Information to be processed and processing required	✓	✓	
Task 2	• Printout of design of the tables • Relationship form	✓	✓	
Task 3	Form design – customised to improve the layout and appearance	✓	✓	
*Task 4		Buttons created to switch between forms: Signature: .... Date:	✓	

	Pass	Merit	Distinction	Checked ✓
*Task 5	• Log of testing • Printout of test data to match the log • Details of any amendment	✓	✓	
Task 6	• Data entered correctly • Records printed	Records PRINTED in order requested	✓	
Task 7	• Printout of search report • Printout annotated to explain query	✓	✓	
Task 8	• Printout of search report • Printout annotated to explain query	✓	✓	
Task 9	• Printout of search report • Printout annotated to explain query	✓	✓	
Task 10		• Printout of search report • Printout annotated to explain query	✓	
*Task 11		• Printout of search report • Printout annotated to explain query		
Task 12		• Source information provided • Data entered correctly	• Printout of search report* • Printout annotated to explain query	
Task 13			• Your own search report annotated clearly to explain its purpose	
Task 14	• Files saved correctly • Screen dumps showing backup copy made	✓	✓	
*Task 15	The user guide	✓	✓	

* **To gain the Distinction grade, you should produce** *one* report for this search rather than three reports showing each supplier separately.

	Pass	Merit	Distinction	Checked ✓
*Task 16			• Evaluation of your database design, showing in-depth understanding of database systems • Clear explanation of problems encountered and improvements you made or would make	

* **To gain the Distinction grade, you should produce** ***one*** report for this search rather than three reports showing each supplier separately.

APPENDICES

INTRODUCTION

Appendix 1	Three examples of application forms; one reflecting the poor presentation typically produced by students without too much thought; two showing alternative approaches; one using Tabs and dot leaders, the other using Tables.
Appendix 2	Forms used for designing a database
Appendix 3	Photographs included on CD-ROM for image stitching
Appendix 4	Mobile Mania Scenario – used as the basis for Assessment of Units 2, 3, 6 and 10. Saved as Scenario.doc.
Appendix 5	Details of the CD-ROM for the Tutor's file
Appendix 6	Advertising material from three phone companies used as source material for assessments
Appendix 7	Timesheets for Assessment 2.2
Appendix 8	Form used to record specification of ICT system – reproduced from textbook, on page 147, and saved as Selecting System Table.doc
Appendix 9 Appendix 10	Hand-written notes used as source material for assessments
Appendix 11	Letters from mobile phone suppliers used as source material for assessments
Appendix 12	Two photographs for image stitching for Assessment 6.1 (Task 5)
Appendix 13	Fix-It Shop Fittings used as source material for Assessment 6.1
Appendix 14	Key Skills Tracking Sheets
Appendix 15	Answers to activities in the student book: Activity (page 74) Activity (page 78) Activity (page 86) Activity (page 146) Activity (page 153) Activity (page 197) Activity (page 200)

APPENDIX 1: APPLICATION FORMS

1A

College Holiday

Name ....
Address ....
Course............................
Phone no ....
D o B .... Gender ....

List the activities you are interested in

Swimming
mini golf
Horse riding
skating
Sailing
ten-pin bowling
Tennis
Cycling

Which holiday do you prefer?

Do you have any special dietary requirements – are you vegetarian?

1B

WHYRE COLLEGE
PROPOSED HOLIDAY
SOUTHERN ACTIVITIES CENTRE

To help us get an idea of the interest in the proposed holiday, please complete this form and return to the Student Office (Room B26) before 18 October.

Please complete this form in capital letters.

I am interested in joining the activity holiday.

First Name .... Last Name ....

Title of Current Course ....

Home Address ....

Town .... Post Code ....

Home Tel No .... Mobile Tel No ....

Date of Birth .... Gender ....

Please tick below to indicate the length of holiday and date you would prefer:

4-day holiday .... 7-day holiday ....

April .... June ....

I would like to take part in the following activities: **(Tick as many choices as you wish.)**

Swimming .... Sailing ....

Mini-golf .... Ten pin bowling ....

Horse riding .... Tennis ....

Skating .... Cycling ....

Please indicate any special dietary requirements (eg vegetarian):

....

....

Signed .... Date ....

Signature of Parent/Guardian if under 18 on 1st September ....

1C

WHYRE COLLEGE
PROPOSED HOLIDAY
SOUTHERN ACTIVITIES CENTRE

To help us get an idea of the interest in the proposed holiday, please complete this form and return to the Student Office (Room B26) before 18 October.

Please complete this form in capital letters.

First Name		**Last Name**	
Title of Course			
Home address			
Town		**Postcode**	
Tel No		**Mobile No**	
Date of Birth		**Gender**	

Please tick below to indicate the length of holiday and date you would prefer:

4-day holiday		**7-day holiday**	
April		**June**	

I would like to take part in the following activities: (Tick as many choices as you wish.)

Swimming		**Sailing**	
Mini-golf		**Ten pin bowling**	
Horse riding		**Tennis**	
Skating		**Cycling**	

Please indicate any special dietary requirements (eg vegetarian):

Signed		**Dated**	
Signature of Parent/Guardian if under 18 on 1 September			

APPENDIX 2: FORMS FOR DESIGNING A DATABASE

Form A: Table in which you must *plan* your database

Name of field	Data type	**If text** – length required **If number** – type required. Decimal places needed?	**Choice field** – if yes, list the choices (You use a combo box in Access to create this.)	**Would an 'input mask' help?** (An input mask allows a pre-set layout, e.g. for national insurance numbers, post codes, phone fields.)	**Is it a required field?** Yes or no?	**Should it be indexed?** Yes or no?

Form B: Table in which you must *justify* your choice of fields listed on Form A

(*Note:* If you have several fields of the same type – e.g. text – you can group these together and justify your choice just once.)

Name of field	Type	Reason for choice

APPENDIX 3: PHOTOGRAPHS

The ski slopes (photo 1.tif)

(photo 1A.tif)

Colditz Castle and rooftops (photo 2.tif)

(photo 2a.tif)

The entrance to Colditz Castle (photo 3.tif)

(photo 3A.tif)

APPENDIX 4: MOBILE MANIA – SCENARIO

One of the units in the Millennium Shopping Centre has recently ceased trading and Tom Chattery and Iqbal Dialup are going to take over the lease and open a new shop selling mobile phones and other communication devices. The address is:

Unit G128
Millenium Shopping Centre
Melchester
ME3 8GH

Telephone (077) 6397 6000
Fax (077) 6397 6001
E-mail mobilemania@userve.co.uk

The shopping complex has been open for 5 years and 90% of the outlets are run by well-known high-street retailers whilst the remaining units operate as independent businesses.

An elderly relative has left Tom with a legacy he intends to use to set up the business. Both Tom and Iqbal already have retail experience. Tom previously worked for a national electrical retailer, Marchants, where he was manager of the television and video department. Iqbal has just graduated with a business degree. Whilst he was at university he had a part-time job with Marchants where he sold mobile phones. The telecom shop – which they are going to call Mobile Mania – is a completely new venture for them.

Their unit is on the ground floor and measures 10 m × 5 m. It has 50 m^2 floor space comprising a main selling area with space behind for storage, a kitchen and WC.

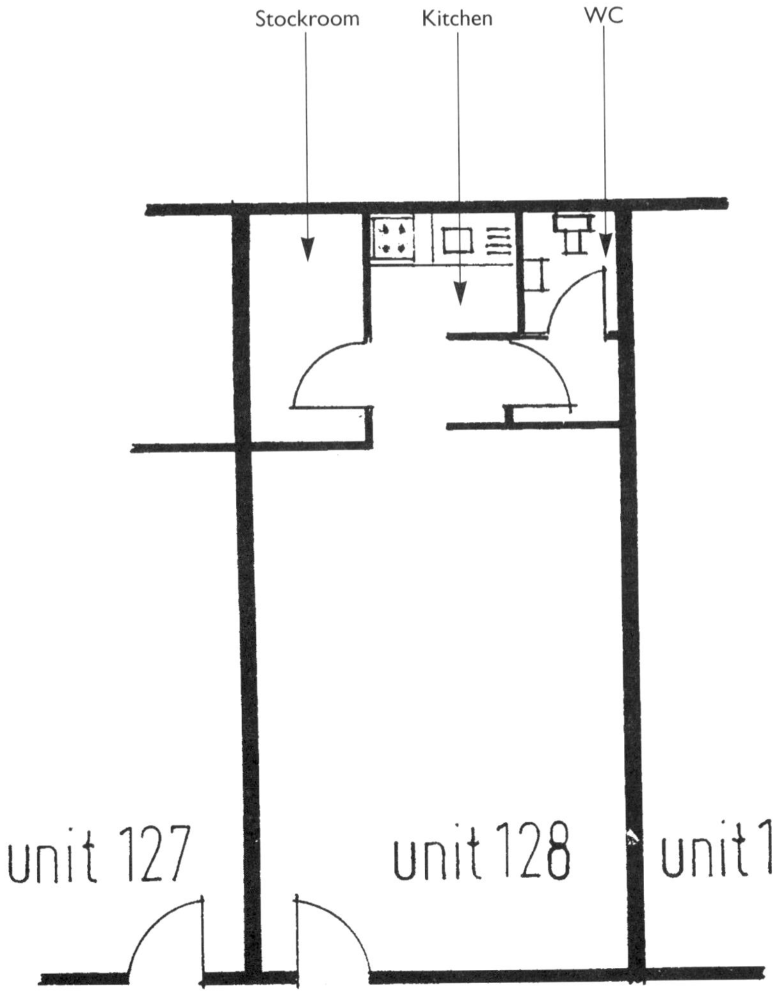

The previous owners cleared the stock but the shop fittings have been left. Although Tom and Iqbal hope eventually to re-fit the shop, initially they can only afford to re-stock it and must make use of the existing fittings.

Before the business can open there are lots of things that need to be done:

- Arrange a business loan from the bank manager.
- Investigate stock and order it.
- Design a logo for the business.
- Design business stationery.
- Advertise for sales staff.
- Advertise the opening of the new shop.
- Choose and install a computer system.
- Set up the computer system.
- Produce information sheets for their customers.

Whilst Tom and Iqbal can do some of these for themselves, they do not have enough time or expertise to do them all and have approached your company, ICT Solutions, to help them.

Following preliminary discussions with Tom and Iqbal, it had been agreed that ICT Solutions will:

- Specify, price, install and test the appropriate hardware and software.
- Set up the operating system and applications software to enable Mobile Mania to operate their business efficiently.
- Produce macros and templates to improve client use of the system.
- Assist Mobile Mania in setting up web pages.

Mobile Mania have set a maximum budget of £2,500 for the start-up. This figure is to include *all hardware and software.*

They expect to use the computer system for a variety of everyday tasks, including routine correspondence, which will include letters to customers and suppliers. They would like to be able to produce a price list of the phones and accessories they stock and display coloured posters in the shop window giving details of special offers.

Once the business is open they anticipate recording details of customers so they can inform them by letter of special offers or events.

They would like to computerise their business accounts and to calculate staff wages.

They will operate an e-mail address as soon as the business opens and would like help in setting up a web site.

When the business is established they hope they will be able to make some improvements to the shop itself, e.g.:

- Redesign the layout of the shop, perhaps increasing their floor space.
- Investigate new shop fittings.
- Arrange for the shop to be refitted.

APPENDIX 5: DETAILS OF THE CD-ROM FOR THE TUTOR'S FILE

The CD-ROM accompanying this Tutor's file contains files needed for activities so that you may use them in electronic form or make your own custom versions. There are also further worked examples.

Word processing files have been saved as Word 6 documents to help users who do not have later versions of Word. The spreadsheet and database files require later version software (Excel 97 and Access 97) for features that are essential to use the material provided.

APPENDIX 6: MOBILE MANIA – ADVERTISING MATERIAL

7_27

Why choose 7_27?

Where else will you get cheap rate calls from 7 pm to 7 am and all weekend?

Whatever your phone requirements we have a package to suit you!

Boxed$_2$Go!

No connection charge. Pre-pay vouchers or top up by credit/debit card. Cheap rate 5p/minute. Peak rate 35p/minute.

Fun$_2$Talk!

12 months' free service and 120 minutes free calls each month. Cheap rate 7p/minute. Peak rate 40p/minute.

Lots$_2$Say!

The package to suit the frequent user. Sign a 12 month contract, pay a monthly line rental and your calls will cost from 2p to 20p. Different tariffs to suit your needs.

Digicell DC163

Talktime	up to 4 hours
Standby time	up to 65 hours
Recharge time	up to $1\frac{1}{2}$ hours
Weight	163 g
Size (mm)	$130 \times 49 \times 27$
Memory	199 numbers
Last no. redial	30

International dialling
Text messages
12 ring tones
Silent vibrating alert

Price £89.99

Boxed$_2$Go

HIYA HY135

Talktime	up to 3 hours
Standby time	up to 50 hours
Recharge time	up to 4 hours
Weight	135 g
Size (mm)	$132 \times 50 \times 26$
Memory	99 numbers
Last no. redial	20

16 ring tones
Text messages
Calculator

Price £69.99

Boxed$_2$Go

Fun$_2$Talk

Webstar WS135

Talktime	up to 3 hours
Standby time	up to 120 hours
Recharge time	up to 6 hours
Weight	135 g
Size (mm)	$134 \times 48 \times 26$
Memory	99 numbers
Last no. redial	8

Interchangeable front covers
Free voicemail
3 games

Price £69.99

Fun$_2$Talk

Digicell DC135

Talktime	up to $3\frac{1}{2}$ hours
Standby time	up to 55 hours
Recharge time	up to 3 hours
Weight	135 g
Size (mm)	$105 \times 49 \times 24$
Memory	198 numbers
Last no. redial	10

Flip design protects keypad
International dialling
Text messages
Portable headset

Price £99.99

Webstar WS150

Talktime	up to 5 hours
Standby time	up to 130 hours
Recharge time	up to 1 hour
Weight	150 g
Size (mm)	$117 \times 47 \times 27$
Memory	99 numbers
Last no. redial	10

International dialling
Voicemail
20 ring tones

Price £89.99

Lots$_2$Say

HIYA HY130

Talktime	up to 6 hours
Standby time	up to 180 hours
Recharge time	up to 3 hours
Weight	130 g
Size (mm)	$130 \times 45 \times 17$
Memory	199 numbers
Last no. redial	15

WAP Phone
Voice activated dialling
International dialling
Text messages
Silent vibrate
Calendar, clock, alarm

Price £149.99

Lots$_2$Say

Bell House, 2 Alexander Street, Brancaster BC24 3PQ
Telephone (061) 7452 7733; Fax (061) 7452 7734; E-mail 727@userve.co.uk

Speake-easy

Unit 19, Melchester Industrial Estate, Ring Road, Melchester ME9 6FD
Telephone (077) 6397 2222; Fax (077) 6397 2233; E-mail speake-easy@userve.co.uk

Speake-Easy phones let you chat anytime, anywhere – choose your price. Free voicemail on all tariffs – if you have a hectic lifestyle check those missed calls at no extra cost.

Straight-Talk

Straight-Talk charges just for talktime. No connection fee, no monthly bill.
Buy your vouchers as you need them or top up by phoning 789.

Cheap-Chat

One payment for the phone gives you 100 minutes of free calls every month for a whole year.
Compare our really competitive rates of 30p/minute weekday and 2p/minute evenings and weekends for any additional time.

Multi-Call

Ideal for business users – the Multi-Call tariff gives you various options ranging from £14.99 to £40.00 monthly line rental. Call charges vary according to the tariff chosen.

Straight-Talk

Minerola MN127

Talktime	up to $4\frac{1}{2}$ hours
Standby time	up to 100 hours
Recharge time	up to $2\frac{1}{2}$ hours
Weight	127 g
Size (mm)	130 × 45 × 17
Memory	99 numbers
Last no. redial	10

International dialling
Text messages
Vibrating call alert

Price **£79.99**

Pegacell PG151

Talktime	up to $2\frac{1}{2}$ hours
Standby time	up to 200 hours
Recharge time	up to 6 hours
Weight	151 g
Size (mm)	134 × 48 × 26
Memory	99 numbers
Last no. redial	10

Text messages
40 ringing tones

Price **£49.99**

Cheap-Chat

Trojan TJ109

Talktime	up to $5\frac{1}{4}$ hours
Standby time	up to 150 hours
Recharge time	up to 4 hours
Weight	109 g
Size (mm)	112 × 50 × 17
Memory	99 numbers
Last no. redial	20

27 ringing tones
International dialling
Text messages
Hands-free car kit

Price **£119.99**

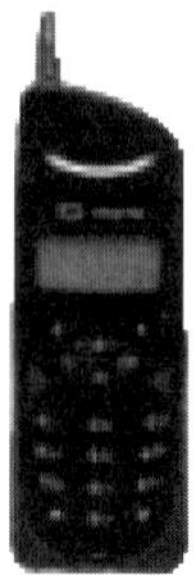

Pegacell PG108

Talktime	up to 3 hours
Standby time	up to 150 hours
Recharge time	up to $4\frac{1}{2}$ hours
Weight	108 g
Size (mm)	120 × 50 × 23
Memory	60 numbers
Last no. redial	10

International dialling
Text messages
Silent vibrating alert

Price **£99.99**

Multi-call

Trojan TJ146

Talktime	up to 4 hours
Standby time	up to 65 hours
Recharge time	up to $1\frac{1}{2}$ hours
Weight	146 g
Size (mm)	105 × 49 × 24
Memory	198 numbers
Last no. redial	30

Vibrating call alert
3 line graphical display
Flip design protects keypad

Price **£129.99**

Minerola MN120

Talktime	up to $4\frac{1}{2}$ hours
Standby time	up to 160 hours
Recharge time	up to 1 hour
Weight	120 g
Size (mm)	123 × 50 × 22
Memory	199 numbers
Last no. redial	20

WAP phone
Voice activated dialling
40 ring tones
International dialling
Changeable front/back covers

Price **£149.99**

CONNECT

Connecting is so easy with **Connect**. Connect helps you to keep **In-touch** and **Link-up** with your friends **All-day** long. Control your costs with **Connect**. You choose the way to pay which suits your pocket. Our three attractive tariffs are:

In-touch

No monthly charge to be **In-touch** and £5 of free talk to get you started. Simply buy additional **Connect** vouchers from any **Connect** stockist or top up your talktime with a free call on 313 from your **Connect** phone.

Link-up

Just one annual payment links you up for 12 months with 150 minutes of free calls each month. Additional calls are billed on a monthly basis.

All-day

Do you conduct your business from your car? Are you a heavy day-time user? If so, you need to **Connect** to the **All-day** service. Check out our various monthly rental options and tariff rates to suit your needs.

In-touch 	**Ring-in RI172** **Price** **£89.99**	Talktime Standby time Recharge time Weight Size (mm) Memory Last no. redial	up to 3 hours up to 100 hours up to 3 hours 172 g 140 × 50 × 25 99 numbers 10	International dialling Text messages
In-touch 	**Tel-me TM140** **Price** **£49.99**	Talktime Standby time Recharge time Weight Size (mm) Memory Last no. redial	up to 2 hours up to 130 hours up to 6 hours 140 g 142 × 50 × 27 50 numbers 5	Text messages 20 ringing tones
Link-up 	**Ring-in RI163** **Price** **£99.99**	Talktime Standby time Recharge time Weight Size (mm) Memory Last no. redial	up to $3\frac{1}{4}$ hours up to 100 hours up to 6 hours 163 g 135 × 45 × 25 50 numbers 5	International dialling 30 ring tones Voicemail
Link-up 	**Talk-back TB170** **Price** **£129.99**	Talktime Standby time Recharge time Weight Size (mm) Memory Last no. redial	up to 5 hours up to 120 hours up to 3 hours 170 g 142 × 49 × 27 198 numbers 20	3 line graphical display On-screen games Interchangeable front cover International dialling
All-day 	**Tel-me TM150** **Price** **£109.99**	Talktime Standby time Recharge time Weight Size (mm) Memory Last no. redial	up to 5 hours up to 100 hours up to 4 hours 150 g 132 × 47 × 31 99 numbers 8	Personal hands-free kit 30 ring tones User changeable front covers 3 games
All-day 	**Talk-back TB141** **Price** **£129.99**	Talktime Standby time Recharge time Weight Size (mm) Memory Last no. redial	up to 4 hours up to 264 hours up to 4 hours 141 g 135 × 45 × 27 1000 numbers 20	WAP phone Free leather case International dialling

Cosmos House, 27 Broad Street, High Wychwood HW6 4VB
Tel (014) 9758 9876 Fax (014) 9758 9877 E-mail connect@userve.co.uk

APPENDIX 7: TIME SHEETS

MOBILE MANIA

Timesheet for month: ____________

Week No: 1

Name: Nabil Mughal
(Please print carefully)

Day	Time in	Time out	Hours worked
Monday	12.00	17.30	5.5
Tuesday	12.00	17.30	5.5
Wednesday	12.00	17.30	5.5
Thursday	12.00	17.30	5.5
Friday	12.00	17.30	5.5
Total *weekday* hours claimed:			27.5

Day	Time in	Time out	Hours worked
Saturday	9.00 13.00	12.00 17.30	7.5
Sunday			
Total *weekend* hours claimed:			7.5

Claimed by: Nabil Mughal (signature)

Authorised by: Iqbal Dialup (signature)

Date ____________

MOBILE MANIA

Timesheet for month: ____________

Week No: 1

Name: Claire Spiller
(Please print carefully)

Day	Time in	Time out	Hours worked
Monday	9.00	13.00	4
Tuesday			
Wednesday	9.00	13.00	4
Thursday			
Friday	9.00	13.00	4
Total *weekday* hours claimed:			12

Day	Time in	Time out	Hours worked
Saturday			
Sunday	10.00	14.00	4
Total *weekend* hours claimed:			4

Claimed by: Claire Spiller (signature)

Authorised by: Iqbal Dialup (signature)

Date ____________

MOBILE MANIA

Timesheet for month: ____________

Week No: 1

Name: James Corbett
(Please print carefully)

Day	Time in	Time out	Hours worked
Monday			
Tuesday			
Wednesday			
Thursday			
Friday			
Total *weekday* hours claimed:			

Day	Time in	Time out	Hours worked
Saturday	9.00 13.00	12.00 18.00	8
Sunday	10.00 13.00	12.30 17.00	6.5
Total *weekend* hours claimed:			14.5

Claimed by: James Corbett (signature)

Authorised by: Iqbal Dialup (signature)

Date ____________

MOBILE MANIA

Timesheet for month: ____________

Week No: 1

Name: Jane Jones
(Please print carefully)

Day	Time in	Time out	Hours worked
Monday			
Tuesday	9.00	13.30	4.5
Wednesday			
Thursday	9.00	13.30	4.5
Friday			
Total *weekday* hours claimed:			9

Day	Time in	Time out	Hours worked
Saturday	9.00 14.00	13.30 18.00	8.5
Sunday	10.00 13.00	12.00 17.00	6
Total *weekend* hours claimed:			14.5

Claimed by: Jane Jones (signature)

Authorised by: Iqbal Dialup (signature)

Date ____________

MOBILE MANIA

Timesheet for month: ______________________

Week No: 2

Name: Nabil Mughal

(Please print carefully)

Day	Time in	Time out	Hours worked
Monday	12.00	17.30	5.5
Tuesday	12.00	17.30	5.5
Wednesday	12.00	17.30	5.5
Thursday	12.00	17.30	5.5
Friday	12.00	17.30	5.5
Total *weekday* hours claimed:			27.5

Day	Time in	Time out	Hours worked
Saturday			
Sunday			
Total *weekend* hours claimed:			

Claimed by: Nabil Mughal (signature)

Authorised by: Iqbal Dialup (signature)

Date ______________

MOBILE MANIA

Timesheet for month: ______________________

Week No: 2

Name: Claire Spiller

(Please print carefully)

Day	Time in	Time out	Hours worked
Monday	9.00	13.00	4
Tuesday			
Wednesday	9.00	13.00	4
Thursday			
Friday	9.00	13.00	4
Total *weekday* hours claimed:			12

Day	Time in	Time out	Hours worked
Saturday			
Sunday	10.00	14.00	4
Total *weekend* hours claimed:			4

Claimed by: Claire Spiller (signature)

Authorised by: Iqbal Dialup (signature)

Date ______________

MOBILE MANIA

Timesheet for month: ______________________

Week No: 2

Name: James Corbett

(Please print carefully)

Day	Time in	Time out	Hours worked
Monday			
Tuesday			
Wednesday			
Thursday			
Friday			
Total *weekday* hours claimed:			

Day	Time in	Time out	Hours worked
Saturday	9.00 13.00	12.00 18.00	8
Sunday	10.00 13.00	12.30 17.00	6.5
Total *weekend* hours claimed:			14.5

Claimed by: James Corbett (signature)

Authorised by: Iqbal Dialup (signature)

Date ______________

MOBILE MANIA

Timesheet for month: ______________________

Week No: 2

Name: Jane Jones

(Please print carefully)

Day	Time in	Time out	Hours worked
Monday			
Tuesday	9.00	13.30	4.5
Wednesday			
Thursday	9.00	13.30	4.5
Friday			
Total *weekday* hours claimed:			9

Day	Time in	Time out	Hours worked
Saturday	12.00	14.00	2
Sunday	10.00 13.00	12.00 16.00	5
Total *weekend* hours claimed:			7

Claimed by: Jane Jones (signature)

Authorised by: Iqbal Dialup (signature)

Date ______________

MOBILE MANIA

Timesheet for month: ____________

Week No: 3

Name: Nabil Mughal
(Please print carefully)

Day	Time in	Time out	Hours worked
Monday	12.00	17.30	5.5
Tuesday	12.00	17.30	5.5
Wednesday	12.00	17.30	5.5
Thursday	12.00	17.30	5.5
Friday	12.00	17.30	5.5
Total *weekday* hours claimed:			27.5

Day	Time in	Time out	Hours worked
Saturday			
Sunday			
Total *weekend* hours claimed:			

Claimed by: Nabil Mughal (signature)

Authorised by: Iqbal Dialup (signature)

Date ____________

MOBILE MANIA

Timesheet for month: ____________

Week No: 3

Name: Claire Spiller
(Please print carefully)

Day	Time in	Time out	Hours worked
Monday	9.00	13.00	4
Tuesday			
Wednesday	9.00	13.00	4
Thursday			
Friday	9.00	13.00	4
Total *weekday* hours claimed:			12

Day	Time in	Time out	Hours worked
Saturday	9.00 13.00	12.00 17.30	7.5
Sunday	10.00	14.00	4
Total *weekend* hours claimed:			11.5

Claimed by: Claire Spiller (signature)

Authorised by: Iqbal Dialup (signature)

Date ____________

MOBILE MANIA

Timesheet for month: ____________

Week No: 3

Name: Jane Jones
(Please print carefully)

Day	Time in	Time out	Hours worked
Monday			
Tuesday	9.00	13.30	4.5
Wednesday			
Thursday	9.00	13.30	4.5
Friday			
Total *weekday* hours claimed:			9

Day	Time in	Time out	Hours worked
Saturday			
Sunday	10.00 13.00	12.00 16.00	5
Total *weekend* hours claimed:			5

Claimed by: Jane Jones (signature)

Authorised by: Iqbal Dialup (signature)

Date ____________

MOBILE MANIA

Timesheet for month: ____________

Week No: 3

Name: James Corbett
(Please print carefully)

Day	Time in	Time out	Hours worked
Monday			
Tuesday			
Wednesday			
Thursday			
Friday			
Total *weekday* hours claimed:			

Day	Time in	Time out	Hours worked
Saturday	9.00 13.00	12.00 18.00	8
Sunday	10.00 13.00	12.30 17.00	6.5
Total *weekend* hours claimed:			14.5

Claimed by: James Corbett (signature)

Authorised by: Iqbal Dialup (signature)

Date ____________

MOBILE MANIA

Timesheet for month: ____________

Week No: 4

Name: Claire Spiller

(Please print carefully)

Day	Time in	Time out	Hours worked
Monday	9.00	13.00	4
Tuesday			
Wednesday	9.00	13.00	4
Thursday			
Friday	9.00	13.00	4
Total *weekday* hours claimed:			12

Day	Time in	Time out	Hours worked
Saturday	9.00 13.00	12.00 17.30	7.5
Sunday	10.00	14.00	4
Total *weekend* hours claimed:			11.5

Claimed by: Claire Spiller (signature)

Authorised by: Iqbal Dialup (signature)

Date ____________

MOBILE MANIA

Timesheet for month: ____________

Week No: 4

Name: James Corbett

(Please print carefully)

Day	Time in	Time out	Hours worked
Monday			
Tuesday			
Wednesday			
Thursday			
Friday			
Total *weekday* hours claimed:			

Day	Time in	Time out	Hours worked
Saturday	9.00 13.00	12.00 18.00	8
Sunday	10.00 13.00	12.30 17.00	6.5
Total *weekend* hours claimed:			14.5

Claimed by: James Corbett (signature)

Authorised by: Iqbal Dialup (signature)

Date ____________

MOBILE MANIA

Timesheet for month: ____________

Week No: 4

Name: Mavis McKay

(Please print carefully)

Day	Time in	Time out	Hours worked
Monday	9.00	13.30	4.5
Tuesday	9.00	13.30	4.5
Wednesday	9.00	13.30	4.5
Thursday	9.00	13.30	4.5
Friday	9.00	13.30	4.5
Total *weekday* hours claimed:			22.5

Day	Time in	Time out	Hours worked
Saturday	12.00	14.00	2
Sunday	10.00 13.00	12.00 16.00	5
Total *weekend* hours claimed:			7

Claimed by: Mavis McKay (signature)

Authorised by: Iqbal Dialup (signature)

Date ____________

APPENDIX 8: SELECTING AN ICT SYSTEM

(Saved as Selecting System Table.doc.)

Component/software	✓/?	Justification for use
Input devices		
Keyboard		
Mouse		
Rollerball		
Scanner		
Digital camera		
Microphone		
Joystick		
Main processing unit		
Describe the type of processor, memory, hard drive size, disk drives, etc., you would recommend		
Backup system		
Modem		
Network card		
Output devices		
VDU		
Printer		
Speakers		
Software		
Operating system		
Word processing		
Spreadsheet		
Database		
Desktop publishing		
Graphics		
E-mail		
Personal organiser		
Utilities		
Programming languages		
Cables and connectors		
Describe briefly		

APPENDIX 9: HANDWRITTEN NOTES OF CUSTOMER DETAILS

Saturday

Mr John Blundell AC 0321
25 Clarence Avenue
Melchester
ME2 8AH

Lots to Say HY 130 S/NO HY 891
No: 07025 567 328
£149.99 plus insurance

Ms Clare Lin AC 1965
49 The Close
High Wychwood
HW6 7TH

R1 ~~746~~ 163 / S.No ~~R1 1746~~ R1 1746 Link-up scheme
£99.99
07038 439 210 Mobile No

Miss Murah ~~Sakid~~ Shahid AC 2178
68 Church Street
Brancaster BC39 1JS 07025 462 167 No.

TB141 £129.99 with insurance
Serial No TB7216
All day Tariff

Saturday

Mr Nimesh Patel
180 Long Hill
Brancaster
BC1 JFG

AC 2769

Multi-call MN120 S/No MN216 £149.99
plus insurance (07018) 276 126
Mobile No ↑

Mrs Sheila Brown
31 Kent Close
High Wychwood
HW8 9RT
Tel No:
07018 289 345 TJ 109 £119.99
Serial Number TJ 1264

AC 3427

Mrs Janice Clements
28 Stow Hill
Melchester
ME6 4JK Phone: 07038 478 190
Straight Talk PG 151
Ser. No PG 329
£49.99

Ac 4893

APPENDIX 10: HANDWRITTEN NOTE FROM TOM TO IQBAL ORDERING NEW EQUIPMENT

Iqbal

Can you phone Sarah Jones and order

2 x DC 163
1 x HY 135
3 x WS 150
1 x HY 130
3 x WS 135
2 x DC 135

and Bharat Patel

4 x PG 151
2 x TJ 109
3 x TJ 146
1 x MN 120

and Sew Wong

1 x TB 170
6 x TM 140

✓ done 15/11
confirm orders
asap

Thanks

Tom

APPENDIX 11: LETTERS FROM SUPPLIERS CONFIRMING CONTRACTS

$7_{2}7$

BELL HOUSE
2 ALEXANDER STREET
BRANCASTER
BC24 3PQ

TEL **(061) 7452 7733**
FAX **(061) 7452 7734**
E-MAIL **727@USERVE.CO.UK**

13 November 2000

Mr T Chattery
Mobile Mania
Unit G128
Millennium Shopping Centre
MELCHESTER ME3 8GH

Dear Mr Chattery

NEW SUPPLY CONTRACT 24367893

I am pleased to confirm the new contract for the supply of Digicell, HIYA and Webstar handsets as follows:

		Trade Price (excl. VAT)	RRP
Digicell	DC163	£ 61.26	£ 89.99
	DC135	£ 68.08	£ 99.99
HIYA	HY135	£ 47.65	£ 69.99
	HY130	£102.12	£149.99
Webstar	WS135	£ 47.65	£ 69.99
	WS150	£ 61.26	£ 89.99

May we wish you every success in your new business venture.

Yours sincerely

Sarah Jones

Sarah Jones (Mrs)

Speake-easy

Unit 19
Melchester Industrial Estate
Ring Road
Melchester
ME9 6FD

Telephone (077) 6397 2222 Fax (077) 6397 2233
E-mail speake-easy@userve.co.uk

9 November 2000

Mr I Dialup
Unit G128
Mobile Mania
Millennium Shopping Centre
Melchester
ME3 8GH

Dear Mr Dialup

I refer to our recent conversation and confirm that Speake-Easy are happy to supply you with a small selection from our mobile phone range at cost price (excluding VAT) as follows:

	Trade Price (excl VAT)
MN127	£ 54.46
PG151	£ 34.03
TJ109	£ 81.69
PG108	£ 68.08
TJ146	£ 88.50
MN120	£102.12

We look forward to receiving your first order in due course.

Yours faithfully
for SPEAKE-EASY

B Patel

Bharat Patel
New Customer Manager

5 November 2000

Mr Tom Chattery
Mobile Mania
Unit G128
Millennium Shopping Centre
Melchester
ME3 8GH

Dear Tom

I was pleased to meet you and Iqbal last week to conclude our recent discussions.

I am pleased to confirm that we can supply you with our products. We agreed supply prices excluding VAT as follows:

Model	**RRP (incl VAT)**	**Trade Price (excl VAT)**
RI172	89.99	61.26
TM140	49.99	34.03
RI163	99.99	68.08
TB170	129.99	88.50
TM150	109.99	74.89
TB141	129.99	88.50

We look forward to receiving your first order.

Yours sincerely

Sew Wong

Sew Wong

CONNECT

Cosmos House, 27 Broad Street, High Wychwood HW6 4VB
Tel (014) 9758 9876 Fax (014) 9758 9877 E-mail connect@userve.co.uk

APPENDIX 12: TWO PHOTOGRAPHS FOR IMAGE STITCHING

(Shop1.jpg
Unit G127

(Shop2.jpg
Unit G128

APPENDIX 13: FIX-IT SHOP FITTINGS

FIX-IT SHOP FITTINGS

187–189 London Road
Melchester ME7 2SE
Tel: (077) 6397 5210
Fax: (077) 6397 5211
Email: fixit@aserver.co.uk

Glass counter edged in beech. Beech legs. Glass shelf.

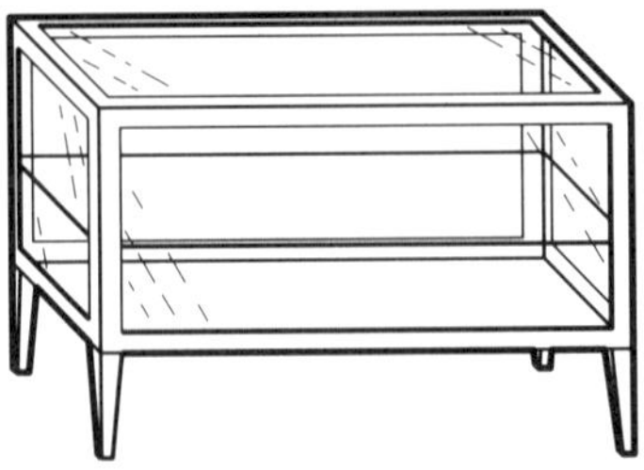

w		*h*		*d*
150	×	*100*	×	*80*
200	×	*100*	×	*80*
250	×	*100*	×	*80*

(*Note:* all measurements are in cm)

Beech panelled counter. High front. Can be supplied to fit left or right

Overall dimensions

	w		*h*		*d*
3 panels	*180*	×	*125*	×	*70*
4 panels	*240*	×	*125*	×	*70*
5 panels	*310*	×	*125*	×	*70*

Beech floor stand. Access from 2 sides. Double door

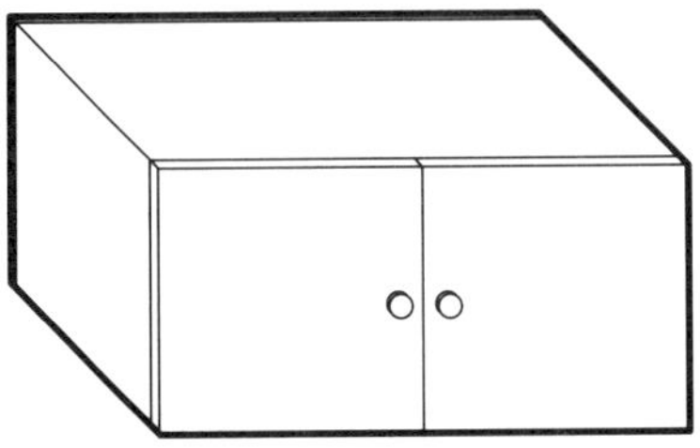

w		*h*		*d*
90	×	*60*	×	*90*

Wall fitting display stands – beech – storage at base. Hook-on fittings.

2 doors

w		*h*		*d*
120	×	*200*	×	*30*
150	×	*200*	×	*30*

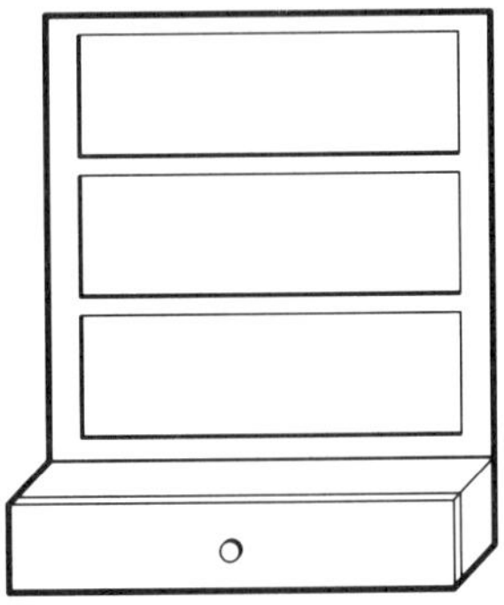

1 drawer

w		*h*		*d*
80	×	*200*	×	*30*
100	×	*200*	×	*30*

Display panel with poster insert

w		*h*
80	×	*200*
100	×	*200*

Wall fitting display stand.
Beech, glass shelves.

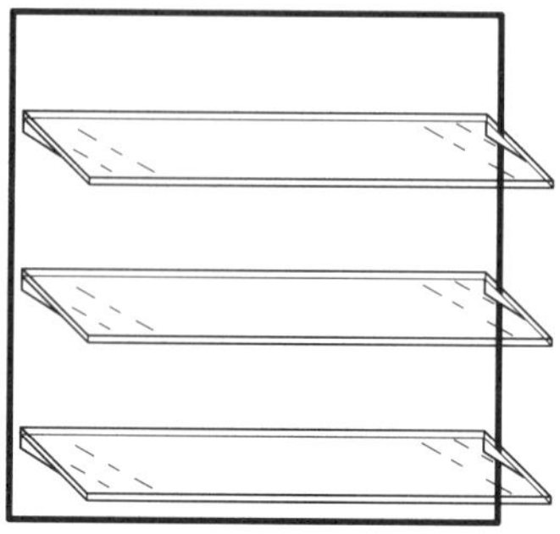

w		*h*		*d*
80	×	*200*	×	*25*
100	×	*200*	×	*25*
120	×	*200*	×	*25*
150	×	*200*	×	*25*

Table – beech.

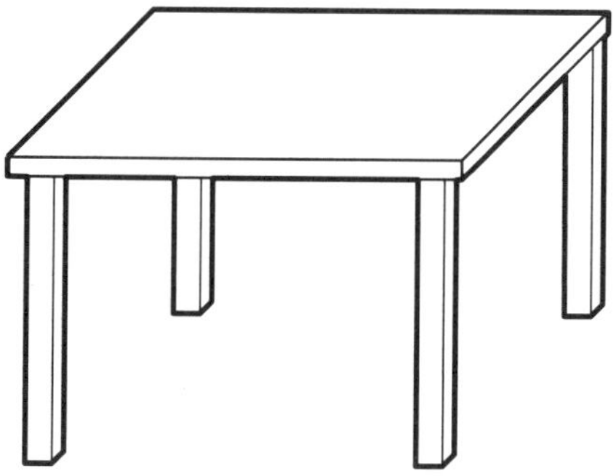

w		*h*		*d*
70	×	*70*	×	*90*
100	×	*70*	×	*90*

Beech chairs.

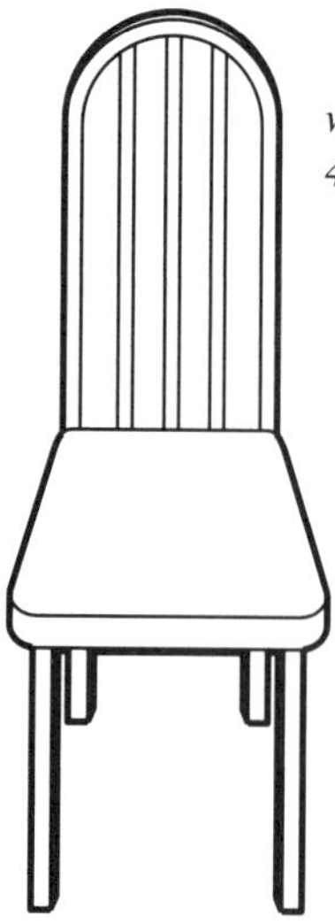

w		*h*		*d*
45	×	*120*	×	*45*

w		*h*		*d*
45	×	*90*	×	*40*

Beech free-standing display.
3 shelves on both sides.

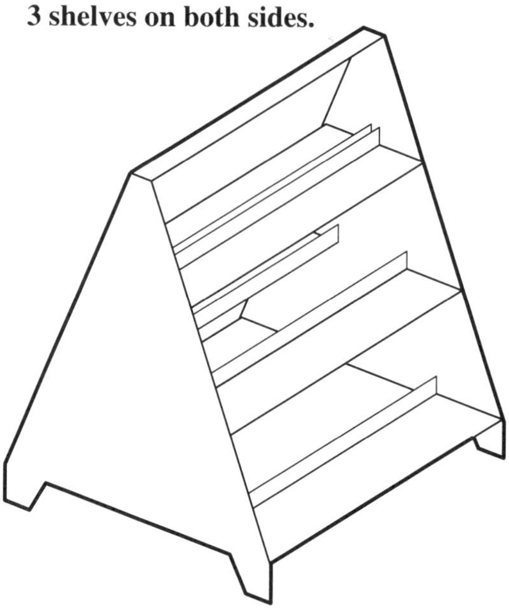

w		*h*		*d*
120	×	*150*	×	*60*
150	×	*150*	×	*60*

Beech floor stand display.

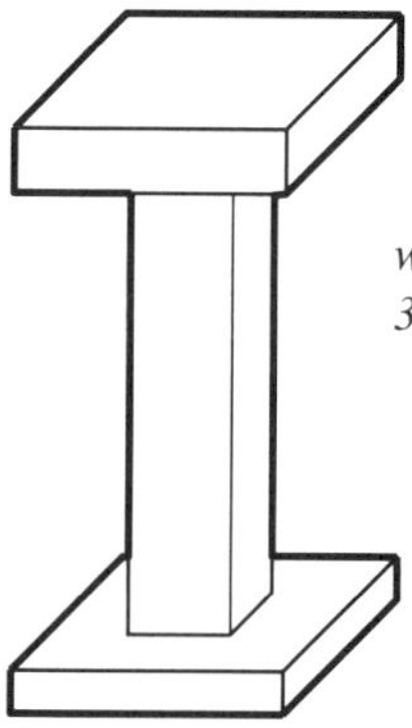

w		*h*		*d*
30	×	*100*	×	*30*

Upholstered seat.
Royal blue or sage green.

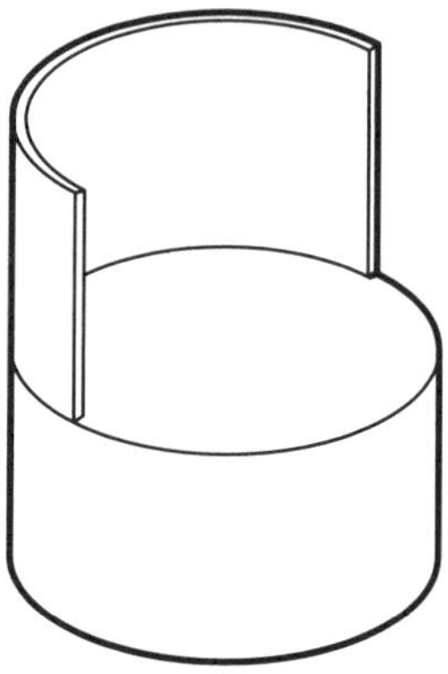

50 cm diameter × 70 cm height

APPENDIX 14: KEY SKILLS TRACKING SHEETS

Information Technology Level 2

IT2.1 Search for and select information for *two* different purposes.

Evidence required	Assessment								
	2.1	2.2	3.1 Task 2	Unit 5	6.1	6.2	6.3	10.1	
Identify the information you need and suitable sources	✓	✓	✓	✓	✓	✓	✓	✓	
Carry out effective searches	✓ Reports		✓	✓				✓ Reports	
Select information that is relevant to your purpose	✓		✓	✓	✓	✓	✓	✓	

IT2.2 Explore and develop information and derive new information, for *two* different purposes.

Evidence required	Assessment								
	Unit 1	2.1	2.2	3.1 Task 2	Unit 5	6.1	6.2	6.3	10.1
Enter and bring together information using formats that help development	✓	✓	✓	✓	✓	✓	✓	✓	✓ Task 4
Explore information as needed for your purpose	✓		✓ Task 5	✓	✓	✓	✓	✓	✓ Task 5
Develop information and derive new information as appropriate	✓	✓ Reports	✓ Task 7	✓	✓	✓	✓	✓	✓ Reports

IT2.3 Present combined information for *two* different purposes.

Your work must include at least *one* example of text, *one* example of images and *one* example of numbers.

Evidence required	Assessment								
	Unit 1	2.1	2.2	3.1 Task 2	Unit 5	6.1	6.2	6.3	10.1
Select and use appropriate layouts for presenting combined information in a consistent way	✓	✓ Reports	✓ Task 2	✓	✓	✓	✓	✓	✓ Reports
Develop the presentation to suit your purpose and the types of information	✓	✓		✓	✓	✓	✓	✓	✓ Task 4
Ensure your work is accurate, clear and saved appropriately	✓	✓	✓	✓	✓	✓	✓	✓	✓

Communication Level 2

C2.1a Contribute to a discussion about a straightforward subject.

Evidence required	Assessment							
	Activity 3.9	4.1 Task 1	6.3 Task 1						
Make clear and relevant contributions in a way that suits your purpose and situation	✓	✓	✓						
Listen and respond appropriately to what others say	✓	✓	✓						
Help to move the discussion forward	✓	✓	✓						

C2.1b Give a short talk about a straightforward subject, using an image.

Evidence required	Assessment								
	4.1 Task 5								
Speak clearly in a way that suits your subject, purpose and situation	✓								
Keep to the subject and structure your talk to help listeners follow what you are saying	✓								
Use an image to clearly illustrate your main points	✓								

C2.2 Read and summarise information from *two* extended documents about a straightforward subject. One of the documents should include at least *one* image.

Evidence required	Assessment								
	3.1 Task 2	Unit 5							
Select and read relevant material	✓	✓							
Identify accurately the lines of reasoning and main points from text and images	✓	✓							
Summarise the information to suit your purpose	✓	✓							

C2.3 Write *two* different types of documents about straightforward subjects. One piece of writing should be an extended document and include at least *one* image.

Evidence required	Assessment								
	2.1 Task 12	2.2 Task 8	3.3	Unit 5	6.1 Task 1	6.3	10.1 Task 15	10.1 Task 16	
Present relevant information in an appropriate form	✓	✓	✓	✓	✓	✓	✓	✓	
Use a structure and style of writing to suit your purpose	✓	✓	✓	✓	✓	✓	✓	✓	
Ensure text is legible and that spelling, punctuation and grammar are accurate, so your meaning is clear	✓	✓	✓	✓	✓	✓	✓	✓	

Application of Number Level 2

Carry through at least *one* substantial activity that includes straightforward tasks for N2.1, N2.2, N2.3.

N2.1 Interpret information from *two* different sources, including material containing a graph.

Evidence required	Assessment								
	2.2	3.1 Task 2	6.1						
Choose how to obtain the information needed to meet the purpose of the activity	✓	✓	✓						
Obtain the relevant information	✓	✓	✓						
Select the appropriate methods to get the results you need	✓	✓	✓						

N2.2 Carry out calculations to do with:

a amounts and sizes
b scales and proportions
c handling statistics
d using formulae.

Evidence required	Assessment								
	2.2	3.1 Task 2	6.1						
Carry out calculations, clearly showing your methods and levels of accuracy	✓	✓	✓						
Check your methods to identify and correct any errors, and make sure your results make sense	✓	✓	✓						

N2.3 Interpret the results of your calculations and present your findings. You must use at least *one* graph, *one* chart and *one* diagram

Evidence required	Assessment								
	2.2	3.1 Task 2	6.1						
Select effective ways to present your findings	✓	✓	✓						
Present your findings clearly and describe your methods	✓	✓	✓						
Explain how the results of your calculations meet the purpose of your activity	✓	✓	✓						

Problem Solving Level 2

PS2.1 Identify a problem and come up with *two* options for solving it.

Evidence required	Assessment								
	3.1	3.3	Unit 4 Project	6.2	6.3				
Identify the problem, accurately describing its main features, and how to show success in solving it	✓	✓	✓	✓	✓				
Come up with different ways of tackling the problem		✓	✓	✓	✓				
Decide which options have a realistic chance of success using help from others when appropriate	✓	✓	✓	✓	✓				

PS2.2 Plan and try out at least *one* option for solving the problem, obtaining support and making changes to your plan when needed.

Evidence required	Assessment								
	3.2	3.3	Unit 4 Project	6.2	6.3				
Confirm with an appropriate person the option you will try for solving the problem, and plan how to carry it out	✓	✓	✓	✓	✓				
Use your plan, organising the relevant tasks and making changes to your plan when needed	✓	✓	✓	✓	✓				
Obtain and effectively use any support needed	✓	✓	✓	✓	✓				

PS2.3 Check if the problem has been solved by applying given methods, describe the results, and explain your approach to problem solving.

Evidence required	Assessment								
	3.2	3.3	Unit 4 Project	6.2	6.3				
Check if the problem has been solved by accurately applying the methods you have been given	✓	✓	✓	✓	✓				
Describe clearly the results, and explain the decision you took at each stage of tackling the problem	✓	✓	✓	✓	✓				
Identify the strengths and weaknesses of your approach to problem solving, and describe what you would do differently, if you met a similar problem	✓	✓	✓	✓	✓				

Working with Others Level 2

WO2.1 Plan straightforward work with others, identifying objectives and clarifying responsibilities, and confirm working arrangements.

Evidence required	Assessment							
	Activity 3.9	6.3						
Identify the objectives of working together and what needs to be done to achieve these objectives	✓	✓						
Exchange relevant information to clarify responsibilities	✓	✓						
Confirm working arrangements with those involved	✓	✓						

WO2.2 Work cooperatively with others towards achieving identified objectives, organising tasks to meet your responsibilities.

Evidence required	Assessment							
	Activity 3.9	6.3						
Organise your own tasks so that you can be effective in meeting your responsibilities	✓	✓						
Carry out tasks accurately and safely, using appropriate working methods	✓	✓						
Support cooperative ways of working, seeking advice from an appropriate person when needed	✓	✓						

WO2.3 Exchange information on progress and agree ways of improving work with others to help achieve objectives.

Evidence required	Assessment							
	Activity 3.9	6.3						
Provide relevant information on what has gone well and what has gone less well in working with others, including the quality of your work	✓	✓						
Listen and respond appropriately to progress reports from others	✓	✓						
Agree ways of improving work with others to help achieve the objectives	✓	✓						

Improve own Learning Level 2

Provide at least *two* examples of meeting the standards for LP2.1, LP2.2 and P2.3.

LP2.1 Help set short-term targets with an appropriate person and plan how these will be met.

Evidence required	Assessment								
	Unit 4								
Provide accurate information to help set realistic targets for what you want to achieve	✓ Project	Tutorials							
Identify clear action points for each target	✓	Tutorials							
Plan how you will use your time well to meet targets, including use of support arrangements for reviewing your progress	✓	Tutorials							

LP2.2 Take responsibility for some decisions about your learning, using your plan and support from others to help meet targets.

Evidence required	Assessment								
	Unit 4								
Use your action points to help manage your time well and complete tasks, revising your plan when needed	✓ Project	Tutorials							
Identify when you need support and use this effectively to help you meet targets	✓	Tutorials							
Select and use different ways of learning to improve your performance, working for short periods without close supervision	✓	Tutorials							

LP2.3 Review progress with an appropriate person and provide evidence of your achievements, including how you have used learning from one task to meet the demands of a new task.

Evidence required	Assessment								
	Unit 4								
Identify what and how you learned, including what has gone well and what has gone less well	✓ Project	Tutorials							
Identify targets you have met and evidence of your achievements	✓	Tutorials							
Identify further ways to improve your performance	✓	Tutorials							

APPENDIX 15: ANSWERS

Activity (page 74)

Justification of fields in Employment Agency Tables

(*Note:* If you have several fields of the same type – e.g. text – you can group these together and justify your choice just once.)

Name of field	Type	Reason for choice
Applicant reference	Primary key – unique	Counter or AutoNumber, which automatically selects the next number in sequence as each record is entered. Essential that each applicant has a unique reference in case two people have the same name
Employer and job reference	Primary key – unique	Unique reference required for each employer and job. Suggest designing a format, since using AutoNumber again might lead to confusion with the applicant reference
Company name, last name, first name, address, town, county, position in company, job title, job description	Text	Text was used in all these fields as it is not possible to limit the choice beforehand and text will be suitable for letters and numbers
Title, job category	Choice	These fields are suitable for a predetermined selection, which can always be added to later if necessary
Position filled	Date	A ready prepared date field is available and, if required, it would be possible to list in date order when applicants were placed
Salary	Currency	Searches can be made for posts within a certain salary range
Post code, telephone	Text	Text used but an input mask designed so that letters or numbers only are possible, as required

Activity (page 78)

Employment agency – plan showing the tables and fields required for the *Applicant's* Table

Name of field	Data type	**If text** – length required **If number** – type required. Decimal places needed?	**Choice field** – if yes, list the choices (You use a combo box in Access to create this.)	**Would an 'input mask' help?** (An input mask allows a pre-set layout, e.g. for national insurance numbers, post codes, phone fields.)	Is it a required field? Yes or no?	Should it be indexed? Yes or no?
Applicant reference (the primary key)	Text or counter/ Auto Number	4	No	Might use text for an input mask Counter/AutoNumber would be suitable, but if used for applicant reference would be wise to use different option for primary keys in job and employer tables	Yes	Primary key is automatically indexed
Title	Text	6	Yes – Mr, Mrs, Miss, Ms, Doctor	No	No	No
Last name	Text	20	No	No	Yes	Yes – might wish to list applicants alphabetically or search for a particular surname
First name	Text	20	No	No	No	No
Address	Text	30	No	No	No	No
Town	Text	20	No	No	No	Yes – might want to search for applicants in a particular area

Name of field	**Data type**	**If text** – length required **If number** – type required. Decimal places needed?	**Choice field** – if yes, list the choices (You use a combo box in Access to create this.)	**Would an 'input mask' help?** (An input mask allows a pre-set layout, e.g. for national insurance numbers, post codes, phone fields.)	**Is it a required field?** Yes or no?	**Should it be indexed?** Yes or no?
County	Text	20	No	No	No	No
Post code	Text	8	No	Yes – LL09 0LL (in Access the '9' allows for an optional number, which facilitates post codes such as SW16 7TY or SW1 9HG)	No	No
Telephone number	Text	15	No	Yes – preset format which allows numbers only (000 9900 0009) NB: phone number layouts vary in different parts of the country, but the number of spaces required is the same – by using the '9' in the places indicated this layout will facilitate different styles, e.g. 020 8666 5467, 01633 623 754	No	No
Current job title	Text	30	No	No	Yes	No
Job category required	Text	20	Yes – a selection of categories could be agreed, e.g. data input, secretarial etc.	No	Yes	Yes – can search for a specific category
Current salary	Number – currency – no decimal places	6	No	No	No	Yes – can search for a salary within a range

Activity (page 78)

Employment agency – plan showing the tables and fields required for the *Employer's* Table

Name of field	Data type	**If text** – length required **If number** – type required. Decimal places needed?	**Choice field** – if yes, list the choices (You use a combo box in Access to create this.)	**Would an 'input mask' help?** (An input mask allows a pre-set layout, e.g. for national insurance numbers, post codes, phone fields.)	**Is it a required field?** Yes or no?	**Should it be indexed?** Yes or no?
Employer reference (the primary key)	Text unique reference; could use counter/ Auto Number but might not be wise if this is used for applicant reference	5 – see input mask	No	Yes – could use a preset format, e.g. employer initial followed by 3-digit number – LL000 (in Access, the 'L' and the '0' indicate a compulsory letter or number, e.g. McDonald's could be given the reference MD 156)	Yes – no duplicates	Primary key is automatically indexed
Company name	Text	30	No	No	Yes	Yes – can list names alphabetically or search for a particular company
Address	Text	30	No	No	No	No
Town	Text	20	No	No	No	Yes – might want to search for jobs in a particular area
County	Text	20	No	No	No	No

Name of field	Data type	**If text** – length required **If number** – type required. Decimal places needed?	**Choice field** – if yes, list the choices (You use a combo box in Access to create this.)	**Would an 'input mask' help?** (An input mask allows a pre-set layout, e.g. for national insurance numbers, post codes, phone fields.)	**Is it a required field?** Yes or no?	**Should it be indexed?** Yes or no?
Post code	Text	8	No	Yes – LL09 .0LL (in Access the '9' allows for an optional number, which facilitates post codes such as SW16 7TY or SW1 9HG)	No	No
Telephone number	Text	15	No	Yes – preset format which allows numbers only, e.g. (00099) 000 0009. NB: phone number layouts vary in different parts of the country, but the number of spaces required is the same – by using the '9' in the places indicated this layout will facilitate different styles, e.g. 020 8666 5467, 01633 623 754	No	No
Contact person – title	Text	6	Yes – Mr, Mrs, Miss, Ms, Doctor	No	No	No
Position in company	Text	30	No	No	No	No
Last name	Text	20	No	No	No	Yes
First name	Text	20	No	No	No	No
Job reference – a foreign key – a unique field matching the field in the Job Table					Yes	No

Activity (page 78)

Employment agency – plan showing the tables and fields required for the *Job* Table

Name of field	Data type	**If text** – length required **If number** – type required. Decimal places needed?	**Choice field** – if yes, list the choices (You use a combo box in Access to create this.)	**Would an 'input mask' help?** (An input mask allows a pre-set layout, e.g. for national insurance numbers, post codes, phone fields.)	Is it a required field? Yes or no?	Should it be indexed? Yes or no?
Job reference (the primary key)	Text or counter/ Auto Number	4	No	Might use text for an input mask; Counter/AutoNumber would be suitable, but if used for applicant reference would be wise to use different options for primary keys in job and employer tables	Yes	Primary key is automatically indexed
Job title	Text	30	No	No	Yes	No
Job category	Text	20	Yes – a selection of categories could be agreed, e.g. data input, secretarial, etc.*	No	Yes	Yes – can search for the particular category
Description	Text	Maximum available so that a more detailed description can be provided	No	No	No	No
Salary	Number – currency – no decimal places	6	No	No	No	Yes – can search for a salary within a particular range
Position filled on	Date	–	No	Predetermined layout ..../........./.........	No	Yes – can search for positions filled within certain dates

* Should use the same categories used in the Applicants Table.

Name of field	**Data type**	**If text** – length required **If number** – type required. Decimal places needed?	**Choice field** – if yes, list the choices (You use a combo box in Access to create this).	**Would an 'input mask' help?** (An input mask allows a pre-set layout, e.g. for national insurance numbers, post codes, phone fields.)	**Is it a required** field? Yes or no?	**Should it be indexed?** Yes or no?
Applicant reference – a foreign key – unique field matching the field in the Applicant Table to indicate name of person placed					No	No

Activity (page 86)

Question 3

If you keep an accurate record of the sales of each type of sandwich, you will discover which are the most popular. Also if few sales are made of some types, it maybe best to discontinue them.

Question 4

It would be useful to keep a record of the costs of ingredients, and any other expenses such as travel or telephone bills. It would then be possible to check how much profit is being made.

Activity (page 146)

This is our suggested ICT system for Ian Duncan. How closely do your ideas match? We should have similar lists but there may be some differences. The justification we have given should help you understand any differences.

Component/software	✓/?	**Justification for use**
Input devices		
Keyboard	✓	To enter text, numbers and formulae
Mouse	✓	To select words and icons
Rollerball		
Scanner	✓	To incorporate photographs of food into the business menus
Digital camera	?	Perhaps to take photos of Ian's dishes
Microphone		
Joystick		
Main processing unit		
Describe the type of processor, memory, hard drive size, disk drives, etc., you would recommend	✓	Pentium III, 600 MHz with >12 MB hard drive, 128 MB RAM, floppy & CD-ROM drives
Backup system	✓	Writable CD-ROM drive to back up hard drive regularly
Modem	?	They might benefit from having e-mail so that some of their business clients can order lunches without having to phone Ian
Network card		
Output devices		
VDU	✓	For soft copy of the menus, letters and accounts
Printer	✓	A colour printer will enable him to print menus and advertising leaflets in colour. They could incorporate a coloured logo
Speakers		
Software		
Operating system	✓	Windows 2000
Word processing	✓	This would enable Mum to produce the menus and covering letters
Spreadsheet	✓	To help with working out the invoices
Database	?	Ian could keep details of all his clients on a database which would also be useful if he wanted to do a mailshot to chase up enquiries

Component/software	✓/?	Justification for use
Desktop publishing	?	At the moment he can probably do everything he requires on a word processor but it might be useful in future
Graphics	?	Useful if he wants to design his own logo or enhance the photos
E-mail	?	For electronic communication with clients
Personal organiser	✓	To remind him when to chase up enquiries and record his appointments
Utilities	✓	Virus checker to protect system from possible computer viruses
Programming languages	?	Ian will benefit from templates of letterhead, menus and invoice. As the business expands he might want to advertise on the Internet
Cables and connectors		
Describe briefly	✓	Cables to connect peripherals with CPU

Activity (page 153)

On page 153 you investigated methods of configuring your computer. The following will help you check your answers:

Change the ruler from inches to centimetres	Tools, Options, General
Remove the Status Bar	Tools, Options, View
Change the desktop colours	Control Panel, Desktop
Ensure backup copies are always created	Tools, Options, Save
Remove vertical and horizontal scroll bars	Tools, Options, View
Set keyboard control keys	Tools, Customize, Keyboard
Save a template	File, Save As, File type – Template
Add a tail to the mouse	Control Panel, Mouse
Change file locations	Tools, Options, Save
Display the vertical ruler	Tools, Options, View
Use a template	File, New, Templates
Turn off drag and drop editing	Tools, Options, Edit
Set a password	Control Panel, Password
Remove the option that underlines spelling errors	Tools, Options, Spelling and Grammar
Create a macro	Tools, Macro, Record Macro
Change backup timing	Tools, Options, Save
Change the toolbar display	Tools, Customize
Change the computer time and date	Control Panel, Date/Time
Ensure days of the week are automatically given capital letters	Tools, AutoCorrect

Activity (page 153)

Configuring Ian Duncan's new computer system

On pages 153–154 you considered ways to configure Ian's new computer system. Did your list include some of the following?

- Check preference to work with the ruler set to inches or centimetres.
- Check if left-handed use of the mouse required.
- Check the properties of the desktop area to make sure text on the menu bar, etc., is not too small.
- Check date and time settings.
- Establish password requirements from Ian and set up if required.
- Check both standard and formatting toolbars are displayed.
- Ensure regular backup timings.
- Set default file specifications.
- Set up folder and file structures so that he can separate his business lunches from the weddings.
- Create separate folders for enquiries and bookings for both lunches and weddings.
- Create templates for his letterhead and invoice.
- Create templates or style sheets for the business menus.
- Create templates or style sheets for the wedding menus.
- Create a macro to insert his logo into documents.
- Create a template or macro in a spreadsheet to calculate the bills.

Page 197 Figure 6.3

Reading each row across from left to right, starting with top row, the road signs are: Give way, Cars only, No left turn, No overtaking, Slippery road, Buses only, Oncoming traffic has priority, Wild animals, End of motorway.

Page 197 Figure 6.4

Reading each row from left to right, starting with top row: Disabled toilet, No smoking, Parking, Information, Fire alarm, Danger of electrocution, Beware of dog, Highly flammable, Water falling from above, Pharmacy, Recyclable, Post Office, Bicycle lane, Poison, Breakable, Washing instructions.

Page 200 Figure 6.10

Reading each row from left to right, starting with top row, the company logos are: NatWest, Virgin; Lloyds Bank, Shell; McDonald's, Penguin Books, Microsoft, The Times; Kellogg's, Wall's, Apple Computers, Volkswagen; Ladybird Books, Mercedes, Bird's Eye, British Gas.